The View from your Cupboard

Denis Shessingham
November 2000

THE VIEW FROM YOUR CUPBOARD

An Ex-Bank Manager's Tale

Denis Sherringham (ACIB)

WALTON PUBLISHING

British Library Cataloguing in Publication Data
A catalogue record for this book is available from the
British Library

ISBN 0-9532878-1-5

Typeset by Amolibros, Watchet, Somerset
This book production has been managed by Amolibros
Printed and bound by T J International Ltd, Padstow,
Cornwall

Denis Sherringham was born in 1929 to a working-class family. As a scholarship-boy, his secondary education was at Westcliff High School for Boys in Essex. When he joined the school in 1940, it was sharing accommodation with the Herbert Strutt School, Belper, Derbyshire, as a result of evacuation. He entered Barclays Bank as a junior clerk in August 1945. It was difficult in those days for young men from a working-class background to enter a career in banking, which was the preserve of the middle-class. Consequently he resigned in June 1947 and volunteered to serve for seven years before the mast in the Royal Navy. On completion of his time, he re-entered Barclays, again as a junior clerk. He eventually retired in February 1989, by which time he was Business Centre Manager of Barclays Bank plc, Basildon, Essex.

Previous Books:

Growing Up In Southend-on-Sea, 1929-1947 approximately

– *Southend On Sunday:* "It is a delightful narrative and for thousands of Southenders, who lived through those years, it will provide a wonderful trip down Memory Lane."

Swing The Lamp, Jack Dusty, or, So I Joined The Navy

– *Navy News:* "After World War II, with strict economies imposed by the Atlee administration, much of the RN Fleet was put into 'Mothballs'. Life in the navy in the period 1945-1954 is described in Denis Sherringham's engaging memoirs. Denis endured his share of life in "mothballs", but there were also spells on the Spanish Main and in the Mediterranean to brighten his time through the post-war austerity era. It is a period that has received scant attention in naval reminiscences, so this one will help to fill the gap."

Author's Undertaking To Purchasers

Every penny of the purchase price of this book will be a donation to the Bankers Benevolent Fund (formerly known as The Bank Clerks' Orphanage and subsequently The Bank Clerks' Orphans' Fund). The only exception will be when books are purchased from bookshops, in which case the normal trade discounts paid to booksellers will be excluded. Monies paid to Walton Publishing for direct purchase will be passed to the Bankers Benevolent Fund in full.

Contents

List of Illustrations

Illustrations are facing page 112.

1 The old branch of Barclays Bank at 108 High Street, Southend-on-Sea.
2 24 High Street, Southend-on-Sea, where the author joined Barclays in 1945.
3 The Barclays Bank Supervisors' Course at Wimbledon, 1957.
4 The "Room" – in Barclays' head office, 54 Lombard Street.
5 The Thames barge, *Kitty*, in the Barge Match, 1965.
6 Ashridge Management College, 1967.
7 Ashdown Park Management College, 1976.
8 Retirement: 1989.

Acknowledgements

Acknowledgement is extended with thanks to Barclays Bank plc, Group Archives Dept for photographs and technical information, to the library of the Chartered Institute of Bankers for technical information. I also thank John and June Prime for the photograph of the Thames barge, *Kitty*.

I wish to thank Dave Keats who processed the photographs ready for publication.

All the above parties provided material free of charge and I am most grateful to all of them.

Denis Sherringham

Introduction

The object in writing this book is to convey to present and future generations what it was like to work for a major British bank in the years immediately after the Second World War. There were many such young men and women whose families, at that time, would not normally have expected to enter a bank in the course of their lives.

The old City of London was owned by the aristocracy, the "blue-bloods", but had been built upon the backs of the grammar school boys. That went for insurance, ship-broking and for the commodity trade, as well as for the commercial and joint-stock banks. Most of this trade had been founded upon the use of Bills of Exchange and Bills of Lading and Shipping Documents. Those employed in the City needed a sound grounding in the law affecting their area and a good working knowledge of the general practice of the trade.

In recent years the definition of banking has been expanded to include the functions of building societies and savings banks. Staff no longer need legal training, and preference is given to the marketing and selling of products. The whole definition of what comprises a banking career has been completely revised.

In the old days, most boards of directors of the major banks were very paternalistic towards their staff, and, although salaries were poor, especially at the lower end of the scale, they were often very generous in giving fringe benefits. The most important of these benefits to most married members of the staff was the availability of Staff Home Loans at a low fixed interest rate to enable them to purchase houses at a time when it was not the general policy for banks to provide mortgages to the public at large. It was a time when the majority of working-class people lived in rented accommodation. At the same time, ill-paid junior staff in many branches were expected to work long hours of overtime, for which they were rarely paid.

Once one had joined a bank, one had a job for life, and only a felony or some other act of dishonesty would normally give cause for dismissal. It was rather like belonging to a club, and there was a great sense of camaraderie, which I have endeavoured to illustrate in this book.

The title of the book is derived from a television advertisement, which most of my colleagues disliked immensely, but which has remained in the minds of the public even to this day.

The early part of the book, aided by a Glossary of Banking Terms, explains some of the technicalities of banking during the era covered, so that a non-bank-trained reader can understand some of the fundamentals. The rest of the text is full of anecdotes about some of the great characters with whom I have worked, or with whom I have shared a banker-customer relationship. Probably the greatest of all these characters was the late, inimitable, Joe Holmes. His widow, Dorothy, has recently given her blessing to the book, for which I am deeply grateful. I am pleased that writing about him will not offend any of his relatives because he was unique, and I feel that his name should not be forgotten. For all his shenanigans, he was a great banker of the old school and the epitome of a true gentleman, when acting professionally. As with my previous two books, I am not intending to write an autobiography, but I can only explain things as they were when seen through my own eyes and experiences.

Although I do not think that I was really cut out to be a banker, in the general sense of the word, and I go out of my way to describe myself as a "misfit", I really do not regret my years with Barclays. My career in the bank opened the doors of mansions to which I would never have gained access, and introduced me to people of rank and privilege who, otherwise, would not have given me the time of day. Perhaps, romantically, I still see myself to have been more fitted to a career in the Merchant Marine or as an airline pilot. The sense of not belonging, however, has perhaps enabled me to have an almost detached view, as if I was an intruder looking into the affairs of a family, unbeknown to its members. Finally, I dedicate this book to the memory of the astonishing number of my late colleagues who did not reach retirement age, or who died very soon after having attained their pensions.

Chapter One

The Misfit

"So, you want to be a greyhound racing manager?" The question was directed at a callow youth who was sitting rather uncomfortably on the edge of his seat. He was being interviewed by the headmaster of a grammar school which prided itself on the academic achievements of its pupils and alumni.

"Yes, sir," came the timid reply, as the interviewee shuffled anxiously on the chair. "I want an open-air job, I do not want to be confined to an office."

The headmaster was a busy man and there were at least twenty more career interviewees to be seen. He did not suffer fools gladly. Curtly he passed an envelope to the lad. "Take this note to Mr Haskell-Thomas, manager of Barclays Bank in the High Street. An appointment has already been made for you, for next Tuesday morning at eleven o'clock." The youth was dismissed with the wave of a hand, and the interview was at an end. That was as far as careers guidance went in schools in those days.

Mr Haskell-Thomas was a man of small stature, balding and had the rather flustered air that was the hallmark of a well-known actor of the day, Robertson Hare. The meeting lasted only a few minutes, and the applicant was given a starting date after the forthcoming school summer holidays. It was thus that I entered Barclays Bank Limited, rather against my will, for it was indeed I, who was the lad who

1

had expressed the desire to be a greyhound racing manager! The idea was not my own, but came from my father, who had for many years supplemented the family income with a second job in the evenings as a Totalisator Supervisor at the local dog track. The suggestion had appealed to me since I did not wish to become one of those that I considered to be the "grey people" – who commuted daily on the eighty-mile return journey to the City. This was usually the lot of my school companions who had not gone on to university, but who had taken City jobs in banking, the Stock Exchange, insurance or shipbroking.

The year was 1945 and the interview with the headmaster had occurred just after V-E Day (Victory-in-Europe Day). I commenced work for Barclays on the day after V-J (Victory-over-Japan Day), 16th August 1945. Like other grammar schoolboys of that time, who came from working-class homes, I was entering into a world unknown to my parents. Until the late 1930s few working-class children went to grammar schools and, consequently, few went into service with the major banks. Banks were not for the proletariat as workers were paid their wages weekly in cash, under the provisions of the Trucks Act. There was no provision for hire-purchase instalments to be paid over bank counters, and so there was no call for non-account-holders to enter the banking halls. Any savings were made through the buying of savings stamps from the post office, or by taking out a post office savings account.

Most employees came from middle-class homes and many had attended public or private schools. They needed guarantees from wealthy parents or guardians. One older colleague of mine who has since died, was in his thirties at the end of the war. He explained how, at the age of twenty-six, he had applied for permission from the bank to marry which, unbelievably, was necessary in those days. His request was refused because his employers considered that he had insufficient income to support a wife and family. One has to ask why a man of that age was considered by his own employers to be earning too little to marry!

I lived in Beaufort *Street*, and this immediately identified my family's demographic status. One army officer, upon returning to the bank after his wartime duties, assumed the position of my immediate boss. He took one look at my particulars and, in front of other junior staff exclaimed, "What? Do we have to recruit people from the *streets*, now?" Being sensitive by nature, this insult only hardened my conviction that I was a misfit in banking. The customers of the banks were mainly from business. Private account-holders came from the aristocracy, the professions or the proprietors of businesses. Very few originated from the working-classes.

It was, therefore, with a stomach full of butterflies that I approached the large oak door with its big brass doorknobs and rang the bell on my first day. To my surprise, it was opened by a stocky, rosy-cheeked, middle-aged man of Dickensian appearance in his long navy blue great coat and a black bowler hat. He was of a jolly disposition and after checking my credentials, he summoned me in with a grin. "My name," he told me, "is Tuttle, but most people call me Tutt. I am the messenger."

As I passed through the door, I could hear the clatter of a Dalton adding machine, and voices of staff arriving for the new day's work. The atmosphere was pervaded by an aroma of pipe tobacco smoke and hot sealing wax. Tutt ushered me into the banking hall, where I was shown to a chair. "The chief clerk will see you when he gets here," announced Tutt, and he strode off back to his duties. I was left feeling like an exhibit in a glass case as, probably mistakenly, I felt all eyes to be inspecting the latest arrival, and assessing what he was made of.

I was soon to learn the hierarchical structure of a bank branch. At the top was the branch manager. His main task was to communicate with the local directors at local head office, which was in Chelmsford, especially about any lendings to the main customers of the branch beyond his personal discretion, either for business or for private purposes. He concentrated on his major customers and left the lesser customers and the staff to the chief clerk. The chief clerk had to deputise for the manager when the latter was absent, but his main concern was running the office, and looking after branch control of cash and other valuables. Below him, and roughly on a par, came the senior securities clerk and the first cashier. The senior securities clerk was not involved in branch security, but controlled the documents lodged by customers either as security for loans or for safekeeping in the branch strong-room. He would also oversee the foreign clerk who kept the foreign till which was stocked with small amounts of foreign currency. In those wartime days, there was little call for such currency, as few people, other than service personnel, travelled abroad, but foreign documents and currency were used in what little import and export trade existed at the time. The senior securities clerk was usually a "manager-in-waiting" and was the more likely to deputise for an absent chief clerk than was the first cashier, especially in a branch of the size of 24 High Street, Southend-on-Sea. 24 High Street was the largest of fourteen branches in the borough, with a staff of about thirty souls.

The first cashier controlled all the cash and supervised the cashiers who numbered about five in the main Southend-on-Sea office. Next in descending order would be the junior securities clerks, followed by the cashiers. After them came the machine room supervisor (generally known as the "OC Mech) whose duties were to oversee the machinists who operated the accounting machines, and the juniors. The machinists were mostly young ladies of whom few had ambitions for further promotion in the bank. They anticipated marriage and future lives as housewives. I shall refer to various tasks that were the duties of branch staff and, in order to keep the text uncomplicated, I have put together a Glossary of Bank Terminology at the end of the narrative. Besides those mentioned there were some peripheral staff, the manager's secretary, a typist, and, as mentioned before, the messenger.

As I awaited the arrival of the chief clerk, I became rather more anxious as one does in the waiting room at the dentists! Suddenly he appeared and summoned me into his room. His name was Mr Pleasant, which rather belied his appearance and rather gruff manner. After a few questions and the filling-in of certain forms including such things as a monthly contribution to the Bank Clerks' Orphanage etc., he sent for the junior whom I had seen bashing away on the adding machine upon my arrival. "Mr Miller," said Mr Pleasant, "take Sherringham under your wing and show him the junior's duties," and with that I was dismissed from his presence.

By coincidence, I had known Don Miller, the other junior, from schooldays. We had last met in the infants' school in 1939. I had left that school on the Friday before war had broken out on Sunday, 3rd September 1939. My parents had moved house to another part of town and I had to change school in my scholarship year. We should both have gone to Southend High School together, but due to evacuation in 1940, I had been transferred to Westcliff High School...but that is another story!

Don, like me, was working-class, but he was not the sensitive type. He had a bluff uncompromising manner and if you did not like what he did or thought, matey, that was too bad! "Matey" was Don's favourite way of addressing people for whom he did not have a particularly high regard. Don really was talented. He had joined the branch only one week before me, when he had taken over from the previous two juniors, Bruce Jeffreys and Eddie Bradford – they had both been called-up under the conscription laws of the time, later to be known as National Service. Coincidentally, Bruce had been educated at Southend High School, but Eddie had been about two years ahead of me at Westcliff. Bruce returned after his two-year stint in the army and married one of the machine-room girls, Pauline Skerman. Eddie returned but, shortly afterwards, he joined a Canadian bank and emigrated to Toronto. However, Bruce and I were to work together on later occasions. He and Pauline remain friends of my wife and I to this day but, again, that is another story!

In the week that he had to take over before my arrival, Don had learned how to operate the adding machine, to list (to add up) all the cheques in the in-coming Clearing (Glossary 3); to operate the Local Clearing (Glossary 4), which in Southend was quite large, being comprised of two branches of Barclays, two branches of Westminster Bank, and one branch each of National Provincial Bank, Lloyds Bank and Midland Bank. There were local exchanges of vouchers twice daily, and these exchanges took place in one of the branches on a daily rotating basis. Accounting for these exchanges of cheques was quite complicated, and the entries that had to be passed through the internal book-keeping accounts of the branch were numerous and complicated. Any mistakes could cause a state of havoc in the day's work, which had to be completed and correct before any staff were allowed home at the end of each day. Time-consuming errors causing such delays were not well received by the staff who were seldom paid overtime. Overtime payments, which had ceased to be paid from 1919, had been re-introduced in August 1944, when late working was enforced through staff shortages as a result of wartime conditions. However, in order to qualify for overtime, staff had to work in excess of one hundred and sixty-eight hours in a four-week period. This was difficult to achieve as no allowance was made for the lunch hour, and a day lasting from nine a.m. to five-thirty p.m. counted only as a seven-and-a-half-hour day. Most staff, in order to be able to go home at a reasonable time so that they could enjoy a social life of some sort, commenced work before nine a.m., and often worked through their lunch hours. On Tuesdays and Wednesdays, keen-eyed chief clerks insisted that staff left the office as early as possible in order to eliminate any overtime accruing from the busier days. The middle of each month was usually quieter than the beginning and the end, and these shorter working days also wiped out the late working periods. At that time, the only extra payment that could be relied upon for late-working was half-a-crown's (two shillings and six pence, or twelve-and-a-half pence in today's coinage) refreshment money, paid only to staff working at or beyond six p.m., on weekdays and two p.m. on Saturdays.

There were numerous other daily duties, the biggest of which was to list the Clearing (Glossary 3). All listings had to be double-checked, so that each of us had to machine list every voucher and then agree the lists. Guess who made most mistakes! It was not that Don made no mistakes, but in any task that he undertook, he was so fast that, by the time I had done my side, he would have corrected any mistakes that he had made, which would be far fewer than mine.

There was a young lady, Brenda Steed, who was only fifteen and therefore a year younger than Don and I. As a result of the war, she had been allowed to join the bank at the age of fourteen, but it was seniority, not age, that counted, and I was very conscientious of the manner in which she would look down her nose at me. Outwardly, I pretended not to notice but, inwardly, I felt every bit the "Stupid Boy" of *Dad's Army*! I really did feel myself to be a misfit!

Chapter Two

Junior Work

One of our duties was to answer the telephone. Very few houses were equipped with telephones in 1945, especially in the working-class areas, and my only previous experience of using a telephone was in one of the red telephone kiosks, where it was necessary to insert three pence (pre-decimalization) for a local call. Three pence was a considerable amount of money, and calls were made very rarely, and then usually in a case of emergency. My familiarity with the machine was very limited. I remember infuriating Mr Haskell-Thomas who had asked me to call a customer on the telephone. "Haven't you got that call, yet?" he demanded as I stood holding the receiver.

"There is no answer," I timidly replied.

"There has got to be an answer!" he shouted. "It is a laundry!" He snatched the telephone from me, listened for a second or two: "That is the *engaged* tone!" he responded with a voice that embraced annoyance and despair.

Most of the staff was comprised of elderly males, or those who were disabled and unfit for the armed forces. The rest were mainly younger women in the machine-room, but there were a couple of middle-aged women cashiers of the old school. Before long, however, the demobilised forces personnel would be flocking back to the branches like seagulls descending upon some tasty piece of carrion on the beach. There was to be almost as much squawking as each re-entrant fought to regain his lost status. This was to be difficult because they had all been called-up at different times and at different stages of their banking careers.

Other jobs allotted to us included putting all the signed post into envelopes and applying the correct postage stamps, and this often kept us late at night. Our manager's secretary, Joan Morton, was a bluff, hearty spinster lady of some thirty summers. She had a loud, jolly voice, which, especially after all the other staff had gone home, could be heard talking and laughing in the manager's office, as she took late dictation. She would emerge with her notebook full of letters, and we had to sit patiently whist she typed them and then, after that, whilst to the accompaniment of more laughter and chatter, she sat with the manager until they were all signed. Joan was an identical twin, and her sister, Connie, worked as a secretary to an official in the local Inland Revenue office. They were as alike as two peas, and on more than one occasion I confused them when walking in the high street. Joan progressed from being a secretary in the bank and took up general duties via the securities desk. Eventually she became one of the first (if not *the* first) woman chief clerk to the first woman branch manager, Miss Hilda Harding, in Hanover Square branch, London.

Waiting for the post was a pain because we could never make arrangements to go out in the evenings since we had no idea when we would finish. On top of that, as I have said, other than tea-money (refreshment money was always referred to as "tea-money"), there was little chance that we would be paid overtime. Even tea-money was paid only grudgingly, and the chief clerk would, if possible, hustle everybody out of the office by five minutes to six. To compensate for this, Don had organised the two of us cleverly. On leaving the office to go home on our cycles, each of us would take as many letters as he could carry and deliver them to addresses within about a mile radius of the branch. Many were quite large bundles, and would have cost a high postage rate. Hand delivery saved the bank these postage costs, and also ensured that the post was awaiting the recipient first thing next morning. In return we would fiddle the post-book to the extent of about five shillings per week (the equivalent of two hours' overtime at two shillings and sixpence per hour), which was the rate we received if and when we qualified. This sum would just about cover the cost of a cup of coffee and a doughnut each in the mornings when doing the local clearing. I must admit that this worried me, but Don convinced me that we were not stealing. "Look, matey," he would say in reply to my expressions of doubt, "we take far less than the value of the stamps that we save the bank. Also, we work unpaid overtime not only at lunch-time, but also in the mornings before we are scheduled to start work. Surely we are entitled to a cup of coffee and a cake in return!" Don was the stronger character and I would yield. It was true that we worked unpaid overtime most days but I still felt uneasy. Each morning, in our own time, we would call individually at the larger utilities – the gas office; the electric light company and the water company – on our way to work and collect the large bundles of cheques which were to be credited to their accounts that day. We also called at the post office's sorting office and picked-up the day's first post, including the head office letters, in which were enclosed the inward clearing for the day. Arriving at the branch some thirty minutes before any of the other staff, we would commence listing the cheques etc., so that the staff would have work ready for them at the earliest possible opportunity. This also must have helped to keep down tea-money payments.

From time to time the bank's district inspection team would put in an unexpected appearance. They would check all the branch systems to ensure that everything was in order especially with regards to staff honesty. On entering a branch, promptly at nine o'clock in the morning, they would check the cash in the strong-room and the post-book. By the time they had reached our post-book, Don had made sure that it balanced to a halfpenny! The fact that the post-book was amongst the first items on their list made me wonder what had been the inspectors' personal experiences with this source of revenue in their early days!

However, our "free" daily refreshment came to an end just before I finally resigned from the bank in June 1947. In about April of that year, Mr Pleasant, the chief clerk left to take up an appointment as a manager of Ongar branch. He was replaced by a younger man, a Mr (Scruffy) Watts, who, to my recollection, never appeared to be scruffy, but was probably encumbered with of those nicknames from school that tend to stick to a person forever. After he had been at the branch for about a month, he called the two of us into his room. "I have been watching you lads, closely. You do a good job," he said, smiling. "I see that you deliver a lot of the post by hand, but I do not see entries to this effect in the post book. You know that you should record hand-delivered post. If you don't, somebody might think that you are keeping the postage money!" and he directed a wry glance at us. "And you wouldn't do that, would you?" His manner was that of a parent correcting a naughty child, and there followed a short pause whilst Don and 1 wondered whether to compound our crime by denying the awful truth, or to admit it. However, before we could answer, Mr Watts said, "Well keep up the good work," and indicated that the interview was over. I looked at Don as we left the room, and he looked away from me. The game was up and we knew it. I would be the first to congratulate the chief clerk for the highly diplomatic way in which he had handled a delicate situation.

The sense of being in the wrong job came upon me once more and shortly afterwards I found myself in the train to Romford and to the recruiting office for the Royal Navy.

Our first cashier was a crippled man in his early forties. He had been a fine athlete in his younger days but he had contracted rheumatoid arthritis and, as a consequence, his back was completely bent over. In the office he was fairly testy and had little sympathy for juniors, especially the less competent ones. As with many first cashiers, he served only those customers whom he liked or whom he regarded as being worthy of his attention, so certainly not those who brought in heaps of coin to be counted. He would mostly stand at the end of the counter looking down the row of cashiers. Out of office hours he smoked a foul-smelling pipe. Although a couple of others also smoked pipes, which were very fashionable in those days, it was without any doubt that the smell of tobacco that mingled with the odour of hot sealing wax came from his pipe. Juniors had to call all the male cashiers sir, and each cashier was jealous of his ranking, i.e. second, third or fourth cashier, and so on. It was reckoned that it took a new entrant seven years to attain the rank of cashier. In the latter days of my career in banking, I had known bright new entrants to take up cashiering on their first day.

Southend-on-Sea, being a seaside town, took in more cash than it paid out as there was no local industry to speak of in need of large amounts of notes and coin for wages. In the summer our intake from the seafront trade was very heavy. Surplus cash had to be sent to bullion department in Lombard Street in the City. Notes were made up into parcels for posting to Head Office. Five-pound notes were of the large white type and were rare. They were sent in smaller packets to the Bank of England. Our main consignments of notes were one pound or ten shillings in value. One-pound notes were placed into packets of five hundred pounds each, and ten-shilling notes into packets of two hundred and fifty pounds each. Each packet was made up by one cashier and then checked by another and both had to sign to guarantee the contents; then the packet or parcel was sealed with hot sealing wax. Long red sticks of sealing wax were held over a small gas jet at the end of the wooden slanted desk behind the cashiers. Nobody seemed to mind that these gas jets presented quite a hazard, usually being left on all day to save constant re-lighting. The smaller packets were then parcelled up into HVPs, or High Value Parcels. An HVP of one-pound notes contained ten packets, and had a total value of five thousand pounds. An HVP of ten-shilling notes was worth two thousand five hundred pounds. Since a very good house could be purchased for around fifteen hundred pounds at that time, it is easy to realise the value of each parcel. It was a frequent occurrence to hear shouts of pain when cashiers dropped hot sealing wax on to their fingers as they sealed up these parcels at the end of the day. The wax had to be allowed to cool and to harden before it could be removed comfortably from the skin. One day, much later in my career, at Hadleigh branch, I was unaware that I was

12

standing too close to the gas jet. I had just remarked how warm it seemed for October when I realised that the sleeve of my jacket was on fire! Fortunately for me, I was not burned. Another dangerous practice was the use of spikes for the accumulation of loose paper vouchers awaiting collection prior to processing.

Almost on a daily basis, especially in the summer months, we would have to place about six HVPs on to a porter's upright barrow. The total value of these parcels would be equal to around twenty-five thousand pounds. Accompanied by the crippled first cashier, who was armed only with a police whistle, we would emerge into the very busy high street. Cars were rare in comparison to nowadays, and most people came to Southend on daily cheap rail excursions. Hordes of trippers would pour down the high street towards the Golden Mile and to the pleasure pier and to the beach. The main post office was in the opposite direction for us, and we would be bustled by the crowd as we pushed our way through it with an "Excuse me, *please!*" and a "Make way, *please!*" as we lifted the load up and down the kerb stones when crossing the road. The post office was about two hundred yards away. When eventually we arrived inside, there was often a queue to the parcels post section and we had to wait our turn. No doubt there were criminals who would have robbed us, either given the opportunity, or if they had known the value of the contents of the parcels, but we had no real fear of being attacked. It was not until the Great Train Robbery of 1963 that the stakes were raised.

Dealing with excesses of coin was another matter. Southend branch accumulated huge amounts from the Southend Transport and from the electricity and gas collectors. Tram and bus fares ranged from one penny up to about four pence for the longer journeys so that the Southend Transport paid in many bags of coin, mostly copper. It would be delivered by an "Out of Service" bus. Nearly every household fed coins into the electricity and gas meters. The collectors paid in mostly shilling coins. It was a task for Don, me and Tutt, the messenger, to pile this coin into neat and firm stacks in the strong-room. The cloth bags contained five-shilling paper bags of copper to the value of five pounds; five-pound paper bags of silver to the value of one hundred pounds each, plus ten-shilling paper bags of the old twelve-sided threepenny pieces to the value of twenty pounds each. Each bag weighed twenty-five pounds *avoirdupois*. Stacking this coin was exhausting work, and usually came at a time when we were busy with other tasks, and so occasionally we were more slipshod than was acceptable to Dave Beech, the first cashier. He would call us into the strong-room. "What the devil do you call this, stacking? If I were to kick that pile it would collapse in a heap!" On one memorable occasion he did kick the pile and it did collapse...on his foot! I won't record his verbal response for the benefit of the reader, because this is not that kind of a book!

Other local branches would often relieve us of bags of coin, at the expense of damaging the suspension of their branch managers' cars but gradually our stocks would increase until the strong-room could accept no more. This occurred on average about three times a year, and Dave had to arrange to send a shipment to the bullion department at Head Office. His usual method was hire a lorry for the day from one of our farmer customers. It used to be an open wagon covered by a tarpaulin. It would arrive at about eight o'clock in the morning, and a team of male cashiers and other male staff plus Tutt, Don and myself would load it. A trolley-full of bags would be pushed to the steps of the front door and then single bags would be passed rugby fashion across a human chain to the lorry, where the farmer and a cashier supervised by Dave Beech, would stack the bags so as to spread the load evenly.

When all the bags had been loaded and counted, Dave would climb in the front cab with the driver, whilst I had to ride the journey out sitting on bags of florins etc. Sometimes, if not fully loaded, we would call at other branches in the neighbourhood and take their surpluses in addition to our own. When, eventually, we arrived at Lombard Street, my bottom would be very sore and carry the imprint of various coins of the realm.

By the time that we had unloaded and seen to the paperwork, it would be about one o'clock, and the lorry

14

would have gone. Dave and I would go to Fenchurch Street station and catch a train that would get us back to Southend by about two-thirty p.m. On arrival he would tell me to go straight home and to go back to the branch next day, and not to tell anyone the time we had got home. He also gave me some cash for lunch money, about ten shillings which, undoubtedly, he would claim as expenses the next day.

Although in the office Dave's manner was gruff, he really was not a bad sort. When we played some interbank cricket in the summer evenings, he would stand in as umpire. On such occasions he was a different man altogether and pleasant company.

One infuriating job that would come our way, usually when we were busy, was to write up a passbook. Although our branch was mechanised and issued typed statements, many old customers of longstanding would insist upon retaining their old hand-written passbooks. They would turn up at the counter and ask the cashier to have them brought up to date, and we had to drop whatever we were doing, and attend to this task forthwith. Often there were several pages to catch up, and all the entries had to be carefully cast and the totals and balances checked and agreed by two clerks.

Every day several members of the staff, particularly the cashiers would send us out to buy sandwiches for their lunches. We would try to combine this chore with our local clearing runs. Sometimes we got the wrong sandwiches and would be strongly reprimanded by the offended purchaser.

All that I have recounted above took place between August 1945 and June 1947, but, in the first instance, I was at Southend-on Sea for only two weeks. In the second week I was summoned by the manager and told that I was to be transferred to Cannon Street Station branch on the following Monday. I was flabbergasted! My dreams of having a "City" job without having to travel to London by train daily had burst like a bubble.

Chapter Three

Cannon Street Station Branch and the City of London

There was no junior clerk to introduce me to the specialities of the running of the junior desk in Cannon Street Station Branch. The name of the branch derived from the fact that it stood immediately opposite the Southern Railway terminus, and this name differentiated it from another branch about two hundred yards towards Mansion House on the opposite of the road. The close proximity had probably come about through an earlier merger of banks into the Barclays fold. My predecessor, a young woman of eighteen, two years older than me, had progressed to operating an accounting machine. As with Southend branch, these machines were Mercedes, all of German origin. They were almost totally unreliable, and were frequently breaking down or performing miscalculations that were most irksome because of the time taken to discover the errors; then all the incorrect work needed to be done again. The situation was almost identical with the American Remington machines. In neither case were new machines or spare parts available. Since we had been at war with Germany, it is obvious why we could not replace or repair the Mercedes machines. As for the Remingtons, the government would not grant import licences for what it considered to be non-essential cargo to be carried in the merchant fleet at the expense of food and other badly needed material for the war effort. The only way these machines could be maintained was by cannibalising the oldest machines. This meant replacing worn out parts with parts from even older machines.

There was an interesting corollary that occurred in 1957 when I was attending a supervisors' (OC Mech) course at the bank's Wimbledon training college. The course lecturer was explaining the various book-keeping machines the bank was then using in its numerous branches. Most branches were by then operating the modern National Cash Register (NCR) machines. "I do not suppose that anybody on this course comes from a branch still using the old Mercedes machines?" he enquired, half-jokingly.

"My branch has them!" came a mild reply, and we all looked round incredulously to identify the rather shy speaker.

"*Does it*?" The lecturer sounded astonished. "Which branch is that?"

"British Museum," replied the shy man, without a wisp of surprise in his voice. The rest of us fell about laughing and the lecturer joined in.

Before long, despite my shyness, I was part of Cannon Street Station branch. The supervisor was a comely woman of about twenty-five. She immediately named me Honey Lamb, much to the enjoyment of the others. The manager had another name for me, Sunny Jim! He was middle-aged, balding, with a handlebar moustache and a rosy red face. He had a very lively disposition and a pleasant manner but, when he shouted out, "Sunny Jim," as he often did when he wanted my presence, I soon became able to distinguish by his tone whether or not I was in for a wigging. Generally, the staff seemed to be much more confident and sophisticated than those whom I had left behind in Southend.

We had only eleven members of staff plus a messenger, when our real compliment was twenty-two, and so we worked long hours. This meant that when I caught one of the unreliable trains home, Mondays to Fridays, it was usually after six p.m. and after three p.m. on a Saturday. I hated it. I had to give up my Saturday sport, whether playing or even watching, except on a few rare occasions when I managed to get to a soccer match at either Stamford Bridge or at Upton Park.

The day began with me having to list the clearing. This was no mean task, since the branch had the account of the Legal & General Assurance Company. Legal & General ran two main accounts. One was for its general business and the other to meet claims. There would be several hundred cheques on each account, and the clearing list for each would stretch from the Burroughs adding machine situated by the street window all the way back to the manager's office, a distance of some forty feet, perhaps more. These lists excluded cheques drawn on others of the branch's customer accounts. All of these cheques had to be agreed by double-listing before the machine operators could begin the ledger posting. I am afraid that I made many mistakes and was far from popular.

Shortly after I had joined the branch, a young lady by the name of Betty Goodall joined us as a new entrant straight from school. She did the double-listing with me and soon became very competent. I soon grew tired of hearing the machine operators (all young women) moaning at me. "What is the matter with you? Betty does not make all those mistakes!"

By a coincidence, it came out that Betty was going out with a boy from Southend who had been called up into the RAF. He turned out to be a young lad who was employed by Southend-on-Sea Transport, and was assistant in the stores to my father before being called-up for National Service. His house had a garden that backed on to ours. It is a small world!

Working in our office especially on the book-keeping machines was most uncomfortable in the cold winter of 1945. During the war, the long glass windows facing out on to Cannon Street had been blown out so many times by bombs that they had been replaced by a fine wire mesh, which let in the wind as well as daylight. The operators would wear woollies and coats to keep out the chill.

Cannon Street Station branch had had its problems in other ways. A short time before I had arrived, one of the

18

staff, the first cashier at the time, had been sent to prison for four years. He was a youngish man, probably in his thirties, who had for some reason not been called into the services. His hobby was cricket and, having a friendly disposition, he had persuaded the staff to let him depart on a Saturday to play cricket before the day's work had been agreed. The counter, being in the City of London, was very lightly used on a Saturday and, consequently, he would agree his till and that of the other cashier quite quickly. He would then put away the surplus notes to the reserve, and shortly afterwards would appear with his cricket bag. With a cheery farewell, he would rush off to his game. It seems that he was so well liked and efficient that whoever happened to be the second key holder of the cash safe would give him their key to put away the reserve, in order to save having to break off from work. Everybody was anxious to get off home on a Saturday afternoon. This, of course, was a serious breach of branch security, for which he or she was to pay dearly. On one particular Saturday, the first cashier had departed with his bag and his usual cheery wave, but he was not to be seen again until after he had been arrested. Inside the cricket bag that he had carried off on that fateful day was not cricket gear, but the bulk of the branch cash reserve! I was told by those female staff who were involved as witnesses at the trial that, after being sentenced to three years in prison, he had told them that he would be after those who had testified against him, once he had served his sentence. For this threat made in the court, he received an additional year's sentence. Whether or not he attempted to carry out his threat I do not know because, by then, I had left the bank and was serving in the Royal Navy.

The other case which caused many problems, to both the bank and to the branch was that concerning a Mr E C Brooker, a former chief clerk of the branch. At one time Brooker was considered to be a paragon of virtue in the bank. In the days of the Blitz, when the bank was perilously short of staff, Brooker stayed late, by himself, in order to allow the younger women staff to go home. He gave up taking holidays because, he maintained there was no one capable of doing his work in his absence. The real fact was that

Brooker dared not allow anyone to do his work because he was running a set of duplicate accounts. One set was for the benefit of the bank, and the other was for the benefit of the customers whose accounts he was defrauding. Whenever any of these business or well-to-do private customers, all of whom were situated near to the branch, required a bank statement, he made sure either to give it or deliver it to them personally. On the odd occasion when a customer was handed a statement across the counter in his absence, he would dash round to the customer's address and, with profuse apologies, hand them their "correct" statement. The other, he would explain, was incorrect and had not been properly checked before being issued. Obviously, this situation could not endure forever and he was caught and brought to justice. He too served a four-year sentence. It appears that he was addicted to gambling and, in order to retrieve his losses owed to firms of large bookmakers, he needed to keep increasing his stakes in the forlorn hope of being able to pay back all his embezzled funds. It cost the bank a huge sum to settle all the claims of all the customers he had cheated.

Do gamblers who are successful in recouping their losses repay the funds that they have stolen, or do they think that they can first win a fortune for themselves? I do not know whether Mr Brooker's bookmaker friends were on hand to welcome him out of jail after his sentence had been served. Anyway, his name went down in posterity, at least until the advent of central computerised book-keeping since, in order to prevent a recurrence elsewhere, precautions were introduced. Every week branches were required to "extract ledgers", an irksome task by which the balances of individual accounts as shown in the ledgers were agreed with those shown upon the statement sheets. The tale of the shenanigans of E C Brooker was recounted on every supervisors' course, to explain the reason for the weekly extraction of ledger balances.

Being in Cannon Street we were in the very heart of the City. By walking a few yards through St Swithin's Lane, past the main banking clearing house I would find myself in the famous Lombard Street. This road was comprised of rubber blocks like flat cobblestones, which had been introduced to deaden the sound of the cartwheels in the London of the nineteenth century. Famous banking houses and bank head offices filled the road, and outside each hung the distinctive sign such as the Barclays eagle and Martins Bank's grasshopper, and many others. Besides the signs adorning the entrances to these business houses, there usually stood on the step one or two commissionaires, decked out like the admirals of some Bohemian navy in their comic-opera uniforms.

Sweeping down along Lombard Street and adjacent roads, Gracechurch Street, Threadneedle Street, and Moorgate and others, were bank messengers by the score, all in their uniform of long navy blue greatcoats and black bowler hats. Back home, their wives, when asked about the employment of their spouses, would demurely reply, "Oh, he is something in the City," which covered a wide spectrum. The messengers would be on their "Walks" (Glossary 7), running messages here and there. At certain times of the day they would be delivering the Town Clearing (Glossary 6).

Our messenger whose name I cannot remember but let us call him Jones, was an odd cove. He always seemed to be rather devious, and like all messengers, he was never there when wanted. Bank messengers seemed a race apart in that they appeared to enjoy a sixth sense when there might be some onerous task at hand. Jones was much remembered for one special occasion when one evening before the staff locked up for the day and went home, he was returning all the ledgers to the book-room, which was sited next to the strong-room in the basement. Fortunately, it happened a couple of months before I arrived at the branch. The branch books and loose-leaf ledger trays were all stacked on a wooden book-trolley which he pushed toward the lift. It was only a book-lift and too small for people to enter, however there were no safety features and the folding door could be opened even though the lift was not there. Inevitably, on this occasion, and with Jones not looking what he was doing, he pushed the trolley into the void! The trolley hurtled to the basement scattering its contents on the way before smashing itself as it hit the bottom. Ledger pages flew everywhere, but most clung to the greasy poles which guided the lift up and down. I will leave the rest of the story to the reader's imagination. It took Jones a long time to live it down.

As in many other institutions, it was the custom to buy cakes for the rest of the staff on one's birthday. This used to come rather hard on a junior clerk whose pay was about twelve pounds per month, and out of which an annual rail season ticket had to be funded. Nevertheless, I complied with the custom on my one and only birthday at the branch, which was my seventeenth. Having handed cakes to everyone else, I took one to Jones. His eyes lit up when he saw the large cream slice. "That will do for my horse!" he said. I thought that he was joking, but learned from the others that a dray horse regularly pulled up at a nearby public house, and Jones used to feed it lumps of sugar or *cakes!* I was not pleased to think my hard-earned pocket money was going down the throat of a well-fed horse!

Lunches were cheap if purchased through the cafeteria of the Barclays Bank Sports Club at 54 Lombard Street. That was the old Head Office building and not the one on the site today. One could get a good "home-cooked" meal of sausages and mash, with a sweet of jam roly-poly pudding and custard, or something similar, for under two shillings and sixpence. These meals were extremely good value. One day, shortly after I had started going there for lunch, I must have joined the wrong queue. They all seemed to be young lads, but it was only when I was charged about one shilling and sixpence did I realise that I was in the queue for messenger boys, who received subsidised meals. I was enough of a prig to feel a sense of shame and to be worried lest somebody had thought that I was a messenger boy and not a "bank-officer"!

Being in the City, we did not handle anything like the amount of cash we did in Southend. Shortage of coin was our occasional problem, never a surplus. On such occasions the first cashier would send me to collect it from another branch. I went alone, and usually carried cash of between fifty to one hundred pounds, if not a banker's payment to pay the supplying branch. I did not suffer the ignominy of a sore backside and a tarpaulin-covered farm lorry; I travelled in a London taxi. I felt very important, especially as I could not recall having travelled by taxi more than about twice with my parents. Trams, buses and the tube were our usual means of transport other than our bicycles.

The long working hours plus the problems with the rail journeys to and from London took their toll of my energies. Often the trains were delayed or taken out of service due to inadequate maintenance. Some of the steam locomotives, mostly tank engines, were over fifty years old. Their boilers would lose steam, and on occasions their fireboxes would drop out! The track was equally poorly maintained as a result of the war. Besides having no sport or entertainment, I could not get to evening classes in time to prepare for the banking examinations. Having thought, upon leaving school, that I had finished with studying, confrontation with the two-part examination for The Institute of Bankers, came as a very nasty shock. However, for some time I had been requesting that I be allowed to return to the Southend area, and the problem with studying for the institute exams, had provided me with a lever which was difficult for the staff department to counter. I am sure that I made myself highly unpopular with my persistent requests, a matter that I am sure would have been recorded in my records. Annual reports were not shown to the individual concerned, and it was not until several years later that members of staff were allowed to discuss the contents of their report with their assessors.

There had been some fun and there had been some happy times at Cannon Street Station branch, but we had none of the capers that I later witnessed at Southend when some of the younger men returned from the forces. In the evenings, especially when the staff had worked late to get either the day's work or the remittances (or both) right, there would be an automatic spate of horseplay as soon as everything was proved. Suddenly the younger women would make a dash for their staff toilet and changing room, and the younger men would chase them as they ran screaming to their refuge. After a minute or two the men would return swinging a pair of stockings over their heads. I suspect that the girls, in a gesture of fun, had handed these to them as a trophy. In any event, the result was well received by the older men and women, including the management who would laugh heartily, especially Dave Beech. It was a marvellous way to relieve the tension at the end of a hectic day. Apparently such horseplay was not uncommon in the bank, and one of my more senior managers, in later times, revealed how, when one young lady persisted in annoying one young male clerk despite his threats, he put her across one of the tall stools and smacked her bare bottom in front of the rest of the staff! There were no official complaints, and even the young lady in question took it all in good part! I have not witnessed such an event, but something similar occurred many years later. Whilst operating from a wooden hut, in the early days of Barclays' presence in Basildon New Town, we were working appalling hours under bad conditions. One young girl junior, who had a whinging nature at the best of times, incensed one of our male clerks with her persistent moaning. At last, when all the day's work was finished, he took her and stood her on her head in the wastepaper basket. Again, there were no complaints. All the senior staff enjoyed it very much, and the girl knew that she had got what she had deserved. Incidentally, her father held a very senior rank on the Basildon Development Corporation, but such rough-and-tumble was taken in the right spirit, and no harm was done.

The renowned Joe Holmes (about whom I write more later in the book) related one of the funniest capers to me, when I was his assistant manager at Stepney branch. It happened in the old, original Head Office building at 54 Lombard Street, which has been rebuilt at least twice since. In former days, the four general managers, as there were then, all operated from the "Room". This was a large room in the centre of the ground floor area. Every day they would sit at their desks, which were situated in the four corners of this Room. Despite the bank's sensitivity about non-disclosure, these gentlemen would interview and discuss the business affairs of the bank's biggest and most influential customers, and could easily be overheard by the customers at the other three desks. They would also interview staff at these desks before appointing them to senior positions or for disciplining, even whilst important customers were present in the Room. It would seem to be such a bizarre way of doing business to modern bankers.

Joe described how, one day, when he was working as a clerk in 54 Lombard Street, one of the cashiers, a polished man in his early forties, won a substantial sum on the football pools. The amount was probably not much by today's standards, but it was considered to be quite a fortune in those pre-war days. On receiving his cash, he went to the Room, audaciously knocked on the door and entered without waiting to be invited in. All heads turned to see the intruder. The cashier then walked to the centre of the room, knelt on the floor, and then stood on his head! He rose, stood erect, bowed to each general manager in his corner, and then left the Room. Not a word was said. He then went to the chief clerk and handed in his resignation, before walking out of the building, doubtless for the final time. That is a remarkable story but one that demonstrates the style that educated people of lower rank could use when wishing to score a point against the high and mighty.

Chapter Four

Doing it the Old-fashioned Way

Bank clerks working in today's revolutionised business houses, particularly those employed in the original banks before other institutions started to call themselves thus, would be aghast at some of the practices which used to be the common way of business until about thirty-five years ago. I think that the same would apply to most of the customers of today's banks.

Bank charges are often queried these days, but fifty years ago it was only the middle and upper classes and businesses that maintained bank accounts. There was a certain snobbishness about having an account, especially a personal account. There was the story of one customer who complained to the branch manager because no charges were applied to his account one quarter. "Isn't my account worth anything to you, these days?" he demanded to know! Customers seemed to accept the charges inflicted upon them, although it seemed wrong to me that the bank should merely have helped itself to commission from the customers' accounts at the end of every quarter, without any notice of the amount that was to be charged. The bank was very tenacious in defending its right to debit the customer's account without first agreeing the charge. It seemed as if it suspected that customers would remove any available credit balance before the charge could be applied. There were no general tariffs available to the customer to give any guidance on avoiding or limiting the commission charges. In 1965 I underwent my first visit to see the general managers, which was the usual formality before receiving a managerial appointment. Some questions had begun to be raised in the newspapers about the ethics of the methods used by all banks in the charging of commissions. During my interview, the senior general manager asked me for my opinion on the subject. "Do you think that the bank should bill customers before debiting their accounts?" he asked. I hesitated before replying, because I did not think that he would like my honest reply. He quickly and impatiently settled the issue for me by giving the reply that he wanted himself. "Of course not!"

The manner in which the commission charges were calculated was bizarre. They were assessed by the manager, or by the chief clerk, mostly by both, in the evenings. They each took a junior into their own offices, probably arranged for some sandwiches to be provided and settled down for the evening. The junior had to fetch and return each ledger tray in turn, whilst the manager or chief clerk took a ledger tray and went through the loose ledger sheets of the customers one by one. They counted the number of pages used by each customer, for which they worked upon a figure of five guineas per page. Six pages, therefore, would create a charge of thirty guineas. Against this they would look at the size of the average credit balance to assess its worth, which would be set off against the assessed commission charge. They then marked down the charge in blue or red pencil against the latest balance on the ledger page of each account in turn. Meanwhile the junior had to record the charge on the charges card, from which the machinists would later debit the customer's account. No interest was paid on credit balances of current accounts. No cheques were permitted on the deposit accounts, which received interest at London Deposit Rate, at a couple of points below Bank of England Bank Rate. If the credit balance on a current account was very large in relation to work done, no commission would be charged. For accounts continuously overdrawn, of course, the full commission would be charged. Accounts which swayed from overdraft to credit would be quickly assessed in the mind of the person applying the charge and an appropriate assessment made. Accounts on which cheques had been returned through lack of funds would be charged extra guineas according to the whim of the assessor. Other considerations also affected the size of the commission charged. Sometimes the manager would recognise an account of an old widowed lady who had fallen upon hard times. She perhaps still wanted to keep her bank account even with a very low balance, but never went overdrawn. The conversation between manager and junior would go something like this: "Should be ten guineas. Poor old soul, she can't afford that – make it two!" End of conversation. On other occasions, he might say, "Ten guineas, but he is doing very well – make it twelve!" All these assessments were made purely in the mind of the assessor.

In the mid-sixties, all these shenanigans were to change. The National Prices and Incomes Board set up by the Wilson administration in 1965 called upon the banks to explain the basis of their commission charge assessment. They could not! As a result bank commissions underwent a critical change. Each bank set up a department to evaluate its costs, so that it could justify its charging policies. The outcome, however, was not necessarily in favour of the banks' customers. The banks soon realised how much they were missing, and quickly learned how to cost services mainly to their own advantage. Thus bank charges and bank profits rose to unprecedented levels.

Bank interest was also charged quarterly. It was calculated by what was known as the "decimal" system. Each evening, staff, usually the cashiers after they had balanced their tills, had a given number of ledgers to calculate, depending upon the till position they occupied on that day.

The process was achieved by extending figures equal to the balance worked, prior to that day's postings, in special columns alongside the balances on the ledger page. If it were one day between postings the figures equalled the balance, but if it was, say, three days between, then the figures would be multiplied by three. This, of course applied to debit balances only, and was calculated only on the pounds, and not on the shillings and pence.

On reaching the foot of each page, the figures had to be totalled, and carried forward to the top of the next page. On change of base rate, or at the end of the quarter, all the ledger balances, not just those worked that day, had to be extended and totalled and converted into a cash sum by means of books of special tables. I am sure that there must have been many mistakes made by some cashiers, but we still seem to hear horrendous complaints of over-charged customers on television consumer programmes such as *Watchdog*, even today. It seems that if the computer is wrongly programmed in the first instance, then it is even more difficult to have the error corrected.

Another duty of the cashiers was to pay the clearing. This was for them to examine every cheque that had arrived in the clearing to see that it had been drawn correctly. Each cashier had one or more of the alphabetical runs of sections to check before the ledger operator could begin posting. Consequently, they tried to do this job as soon as the juniors had listed and agreed the clearing, and before the branch opened its doors.

I was introduced to the banking examinations of the Institute of Bankers (now the Chartered Institute of Bankers) almost immediately. This meant either attending evening classes at the local technical college, or taking a correspondence course, usually through the Rapid Results College. The latter would send its representatives around the branches in late August to pick up the latest intake from schools, and sign them up before they enrolled with night classes.

Classes ran from early September until March or April of the following year, when the exams were held, usually at the technical college. In some remote areas, however, exams were taken after hours in a branch of one of the clearing banks, with staff from all the local banks sitting together. Invigilators who were usually senior staff who held the AIB certificate supervised exams. Part I of these exams was mainly on subjects that might have been taught at school, such as, Commercial Geography, English, Book-keeping, but Law Relating To Bills of Exchange and Economics were rather new ground for most of us. Part II was more demanding, and it could not be started until Part I had been completed. Part II consisted of the following subjects: Monetary Theory and Practice; Commercial Law; Finance of Foreign Trade and Foreign Exchange; Accountancy and The Practice of Banking. Upon completing these exams students became Associates of the Institute of Bankers, or AIBs. This achievement was rated as the equivalent to a second class degree.

Our local evening classes in the technical college were held in very old-fashioned classrooms with wooden school desks, in the rather dilapidated building. The teachers were mainly managers, chief or senior clerks, who had obtained their AIB. It was a way for many of them to supplement their incomes, which were not particularly special, even at the higher levels. Also assisting were some schoolteachers for non-banking subjects such as Commercial Geography and English. In our class, Law Relating to Banking and Commercial Law were taught by a young barrister by the name of Gordon Rice who had been in the sixth form and a prefect at my grammar school when I had joined it in 1940. He had gone to university, before qualifying as a barrister. I met him again at a recent Old Boys' reunion, and he is now in his seventies and has recently retired as a High Court judge. I remember his droll sense of humour, typical of the legal profession. When talking about titles to land, and real estate, he would write in chalk across the blackboard, "Black Acre" to make it represent a plot of land to be the discussion topic for that evening. Although I went as regularly as I could to evening classes, I made very little headway in that first year, but that was not entirely my fault. Cannon Street Station branch had done its best to get me away early to catch my train on class nights, as they were obliged to do, but as I've described, the trains were very unreliable, and I was very tired and hungry by the time I arrived at the college. Gradually I despaired and began to realise that it was all a wasted effort, and my thoughts became more centred on leaving the bank.

When I returned to Southend branch, life became even more intolerable. The branch was now full of demobilised servicemen. They were all vying against each other to regain their former status and promotion in the bank and I could foresee little hope for the future.

Although all my friends queried my judgement, as I did myself, it was with feelings of relief, despite a sense of foreboding, that I walked out of the bank, for what I felt sure was to be the last time as an employee, in mid-June 1947.

Chapter Five

Seven Years Later
Return to Banking: Low Salaries

At the beginning of this narrative, I expressly stated that it is not intended to be an autobiography. Since banking over the years covered is seen mainly through my eyes, I feel that it is essential to inform the reader why I had returned to it after my period in the navy. I had done so despite my avowed intention to give up all thoughts of making banking my career, and despite sensing myself to be a misfit when I had walked away from banking in 1947.

It was one of those funny twists of fate that I had ever entered Barclays, especially on two occasions. Twice I had nearly gone to Lloyds Bank, and that bank will never appreciate what a narrow escape it had when, on each occasion, I had been diverted to Barclays. The first occasion was in 1945 when, after being told to report to Barclays by my school headmaster, I had related the story to my Saturday job employer. Mr Marsh, a kindly gentleman, together with his caring wife, ran a combined newspaper shop and a retail and wholesale sweets' business. For most of the war years, I had worked every Saturday and Sunday mornings delivering morning newspapers. By 1945 I was not only delivering papers, but had graduated to collecting the paper money from the customers on Saturday mornings and then to cleaning out all the canaries, prize rabbits and hens belonging to the Marsh family on Saturday afternoons. Mr Marsh was a keen member of the Fur and Feather Club. At that time I was earning about seventeen shillings and sixpence per week, which was more than many a lad who had left school at the age of fourteen could have expected for a week's wages.

The first reaction of Mr and Mrs Marsh was to write a letter of recommendation to their bank manager at Lloyds in Southend High Street. Unfortunately, before I could consider taking it to Lloyds Bank, I had to refer the matter back to my headmaster. He refused to give me time off to attend an interview at Lloyds saying that he had arranged for another lad from my class, Tony Maynard, to go to Lloyds, and he was neither able, nor willing to alter these arrangements. Tony did in fact join Lloyds.

The second occasion when I contemplated joining that bank came at about eighteen months before I was due to leave the Royal Navy. I was wondering what career to take up when going back to civilian life. Being married, my wife was not keen for me to remain in the navy, because it was not uncommon for a ship to be sent to a foreign station for a period of two and a half years. If we were to have more babies it would not be practical for my wife to join me on the station. Besides, ships were often cruising away from their foreign bases and were absent for long periods, leaving lonely wives to while away their time far from home and family. Another factor was that the navy was being rapidly reduced, and I could foresee no career prospects in the long term if I were to stay in the service. One option open to me was British Overseas Airways and British European Airways – in those days separate entities – which were both advertising for flight-deck recruits for training as pilots, navigators, etc. The age limit was twenty-six years, and as I would have been twenty-five at time of discharge, with the necessary academic qualifications, it was a possibility. I talked it over with my wife, but we realised that it could mean long periods of separation again, which neither of us really wanted. The breakthrough came when one day a notice was received on board my ship that Lloyds Bank was looking for staff from the services who had reached School

Certificate level, which was a grade below my matriculation. At the time, I was living ashore in Glasgow whilst storing a brand new destroyer, HMS *Delight*, which was finishing construction in Fairfields' Ship Builders' Yard. She was expected to be commissioned in the spring or summer of 1953, but she was not eventually commissioned until the November of that year, having been delayed because of one or two of the problems which often occur in ship-building. Having seen this notice, I wrote to Lloyds pointing out my previous banking experience and advising them that I was due to be demobilised in June of 1954. As soon as she was commissioned, HMS *Delight* had been ordered to proceed immediately to the Mediterranean, to be based at Malta. I could not expect to return to England before April or May 1954, so, under the circumstances, I asked if Lloyds would be prepared to interview me before we sailed, to see if they could offer me a position upon my return to civilian life. It did not seem to be an unreasonable request, but they turned it down, suggesting that I contact them again once I had returned to Britain in 1954. I was rather disappointed at their attitude, but I decided that I would try to return to banking as I could not see any other avenues open to me when starting a career so late. The attraction of the security of a career in a large bank, which in those days offered a job for life provided one did not blot one's copybook, was important to me. For this reason, I decided to take advantage of the vocational courses available to those servicemen who were within one year of their discharge, planned to assist them in finding employment in civilian work. These courses ranged from driving lessons for would-be chauffeurs, through training in skills such as bricklaying, engineering, etc., to courses by correspondence for the professions. I applied for correspondence courses in Part I of the Institute of Bankers' examinations. Upon being accepted, I took lessons in three of the Part I subjects, and received an independent tutor for each. As the subjects that I decided to get under my belt first were English (designed for commercial use) and Commercial Geography and Economics, none of my tutors were bankers. Most were teachers and ex-commissioned officers, and I developed quite a close relationship with them, but the ex-army colonel who supervised my English course did not appreciate my rather anti-establishment approach to many of the subjects set for my essays. This was before the "social revolution" of the 1960s.

I set myself the task of catching up on all my colleagues-to-be in the bank, who had a five-year start on me. However, I still had no thoughts of progressing beyond the level of branch cashier. I was still thinking of joining Lloyds when I was home on leave, shortly before HMS *Delight* was commissioned. One morning I was strolling down Southend High Street when I met Geoff Ainsworth whom I had previously known as a cashier who had returned from the services just before I had joined the navy. He was then the first cashier at 24 High Street, and I told him of my intentions, but that I was frustrated with Lloyds for not agreeing to offer me a job before the ship sailed.

"Why not apply to Barclays?" he asked. "After all, the devil you know is better than the devil you don't know!"

I decided to follow up his reasoning, and I had to act quickly because my leave was for two weeks only. Barclays responded with alacrity, and I was invited to see a Mr Darvill, District Manager, at Chelmsford Local Head Office. Mr Darvill was an exceptionally approachable man. He fully understood my problem, having himself joined Barclays as a late entrant at the age of twenty-five. He had come from Southern Rhodesia Railways as it was then known. At the end of our interview he promised to write to me confirming the offer of a job but suggested that I should contact them again at Local Head Office upon my return to Southend approximately nine months later; he was true to his word. By the time that I reported to Chelmsford Local Head Office at the end of my naval career, Mr Darvill had become a general manager of the bank. It was, however, thanks to his wisdom and understanding, that I had been able to sail off to the Mediterranean with even more determination to pass those exams, being confident that I had a job waiting for me.

When I returned it was to the small country branch mentioned before, at Hadleigh, Essex, which is not to be confused with Hadleigh, Suffolk, a mistake which the postman often made with the branch's post. If the Head Office Letter bag were switched between the two branches it would cause problems for both the branches and for their customers. One disappointment was that the accountant at Hadleigh was one of the returning army officers, whom I had left the bank to escape! "Accountant" was the title given to the chief clerk position in a small branch with less than about eight staff overall. Hadleigh, which was situated just outside the Borough of Southend-on-Sea, had about six staff. A branch with about five staff or less would be under a clerk-in-charge, with no manager, but would come within the responsibility of the manager of a nearby larger parent branch, as its satellite.

I think that the accountant was no more pleased to see me than I was to see him. Once again I had to be the junior, stepping into the shoes of the previous junior who had left to do his National Service, but this time, instead of his being older than me, he had been seven years younger. The bank was very good to me in that it assessed my seniority to commence from 1950, allowing my previous service to stand, plus two years for my National Service. This seniority helped in many ways, especially when seniority gave preference of choice for such things as holidays. What did hurt was the salary of about six hundred and sixty pounds per year. By comparison with what I earned as a naval petty officer with married and other allowances, I was much worse off. The only compensation was that I was in a job that offered a reasonable pension at the age of sixty-five. In fact, had my seniority commenced before 1950, my pensionable age would have commenced at sixty. However, the pension age of sixty-five was to revert to sixty, with an option to go on to sixty-five, when Barclays merged with Martins Bank in 1970.

In 1954 we had our first child who was just three months old when I restarted my banking career but we had a second child on the way, and I relied very much upon my retainer from the navy. I had signed on for seven years with the fleet and for five years on the reserve. This meant that I could be called back for a two-week training period every year, or, in case of emergency, for full-time service as many men had been during the Korean War. The redeeming feature was the fact that I received a quarterly warrant for about ten pounds ten shillings which obligingly covered my electricity bill! Before I had returned, and at Mr Darvill's suggestion, I had asked the navy if I could buy myself out of this commitment. The bank did not really wish to have to release me for the two-week training periods, although many members of the staff, especially those in the Territorial Army, had to go to camp regularly. The navy refused my request, and so I was really incensed when, upon the change of government, the new administration rearranged the legislation so that the calling back for training fortnights was cancelled. In times of national emergency, however, the obligation of recall for such training periods or for full-time service remained, though the quarterly payment of a retainer was cancelled. Thus I was about forty-two pounds per annum worse off on an annual salary of only six hundred and sixty pounds. I remember how hard times were. My wife and I struggled to pay our bills, even though we were living for a nominal rent in half of my parents' house. It was typical of the bank inspectors in those days, to examine the staff accounts very carefully to look for any possible irregularities, which could mean that a dishonest member of the staff was defrauding the bank or its customers. One month my electricity bill arrived on pay day. To avoid any risk of the money being used for any other purpose, I went to the Electricity Board office in Hadleigh during my lunch hour and paid the account with a cheque for the full quarterly bill. The Electricity Board paid all their accounts, which were domiciled with our Brentwood branch, into the branches local to their offices at around bank closing time, which in those days was three p.m. Therefore my cheque was drawn, presented and debited to my account on the same day, pay day. The inspectors, who had arrived at the branch that morning, immediately jumped upon this. I was called into the manager's office and grilled about my finances. Was I behind with my payments to the electricity? To whom else was I in debt, perhaps to the gas board? They were very reluctant to accept my explanations and reassurances. Eventually they let me go, but they gave the impression that they were disappointed, rather like a jackals deprived of their prey, and they appeared still to harbour suspicions that I must have been guilty of some form of embezzlement.

In the 1950s Hadleigh had no business machines of any kind, not even an adding machine, until in my second spell at Hadleigh some two years later, when the Mechanisation Department, had sent Barry Burge to "install" a Dalton adding machine. Consequently all ledgers, statements, the inward clearing and remittances, plus the weekly extraction of ledgers had to be hand-written and cast by the clerks.

Amongst my duties other than those normally assigned to a junior, I had to stoke the boiler that provided the hot water and heated the radiators, and which was situated in the basement. This was a tiresome task and involved continually interrupting one's work to run downstairs to put more coke into the furnace. It was a temptation to build it right up so that it would last for an hour or two. On one particular morning, I had done just that when, after about half an hour, the manager, a friendly but rather volatile Welshman, emerged from his office in a frenzy followed by a cloud of steam. The radiator in the manager's room was the first on the system, and steam was gushing forth. I was sent haring down the stairs to dampen down the furnace. Fortunately this had occurred before opening time and no customers received the equivalent of a free Turkish bath during their interview with Mr Rhys. From then on I was far more careful in my stoking task.

In all, following my return, I had three spells at Hadleigh. My first spell ended after six months when I was transferred back to 24 High Street, Southend-on-Sea. This was still the senior branch in the area, and where, after about six months as junior alongside a younger man who had just returned from National Service, I was to take up cashiering and other more senior duties.

Other than by promotion, all pay was linked to the age of a member of staff. It was not until much later that "Rate for the Job" was introduced. As a result some older staff, who were either lacking any ambition or who were inefficient, were being paid far more than younger, brighter and more industrious members. It was very unfair, especially, as I have already mentioned, the older staff had priority in many ways over their juniors despite, in many cases, their lack of ability or of effort. In those days the only salary increases were by way of the annual birthday rises, according to the scale laid down in Head Office Instructions. In addition to this, there were what were known as Merit Rises, which could not exceed ten pounds per annum. Sometimes five pounds per year was granted as if the bank had been ultra generous. One had to have done something very grave, or to have been totally incompetent to have the annual birthday rise stopped, but, equally, one needed to have performed miracles to get a merit rise, and eyebrows were raised amongst other staff if one was awarded. The manager sent in staff reports on all his staff, but in none, except the rarest of cases, would the member of staff see the report. There was no question of there being a staff interview before the report was sent to the local directors, as I stated earlier. Merit rises appeared from out of the blue, as a complete surprise, and one was expected to thank the manager most graciously, especially if one hoped to get another the following year!

Because my wife is Cornish and comes from Penzance, I learned a great deal about life for the staff of the Cornish branches under the control of Colonel B, who was senior local director.

Cornish people lived generally on a lower standard of wages than much of the rest of the country, and the colonel did not agree to his staff earning the national salary scale. I have been told that he controlled the salaries by not granting the annual birthday rise as a right of the staff. He manipulated the system so that the annual birthday rise was the equivalent to a merit rise, given only against special commendation from the branch manager, and certainly not annually. Colonel B lived on an estate near Newlyn, the well-known fishing community to the west of Penzance, and he travelled daily by train from the Penzance terminus of the old Great Western Railway to the local Head Office at

Truro. In later years a local head office was established in Penzance. It seems that he did review staff annual reports with certain members of staff, perhaps those with a particularly good report to whom he was going to award the annual birthday rise, or to any who were to be given promotion. To save his valuable time, he would conduct most of these interviews in his first-class compartment on the train. Most Cornish express trains did, and still do, call at nearly every station between Penzance and Saltash, in either direction. The express part of the journeys was between Plymouth and London, with the only stop being at Exeter. Therefore, Colonel B would arrange for his first interview to be for a member of the Penzance branch staff who would travel with him to St Erth, where the interviewee would leave the train and take the bus or train back to Penzance. The next interview would take place between St Erth and Camborne, and so on and so on until the colonel arrived at Truro. Whether or not he conducted similar interviews on his way home, I do not know for sure.

Life was particularly difficult for staff because of the fact that before the introduction of the Clerical Work Improvement Programme, or CWIP, as it was generally called, there was no way to measure the number of staff required to run a branch. The usual system was for a branch manager to request additional staff as and when he felt an increase was necessary. Managers, however, were caught between two considerations. First, the seniority of a branch was usually governed by the number of staff employed, and the greater the number of staff, the greater the status of the manager, and, hopefully, the greater his salary. On the other hand, his worth as a branch manager was often judged by the size of the branch "profits". These "profits" were highly subjective, and in no way gave a true picture of the branch's profitability, but these illusory figures were mainly the basis for establishing the manager's salary. Thus many managers did not wish to increase the branch salaries and wages commitments to be offset against these fictitious profits.

Local directors who were based in the local head offices would also visit branches and interview employees and sometimes the feedback would be that the staff were under pressure. The most common method of assessing the need for more staff was the daily Appearance Book, where staff signed on and off. If the average going home time was before five p.m. then there was no chance of extra staff, despite whatever pressures the counter staff might have to sustain whilst the branch was open for business. Some wealthy customers could occasionally influence the local directors, if they complained about poor customer service, which, in their opinion, was as a result of inadequate staffing.

Consideration was seldom given for seasonal fluctuation in a branch's business. In seaside resorts such as Southend-on-Sea, the summer trade for those branches nearest to the sea could be many times greater than the winter trade, but it was generally thought that such branches could leave non-urgent jobs in the summer months and catch up on them in the winter months.

Some districts were ruthless. One highly popular branch in the West Country had enormous staffing problems in the summer months, but the branch was staffed according to the requirements of the other seven months of the year. The local head office would not carry relief staff to feed into branches at peak periods, as the local directors did not want to carry extra staff for the rest of the year. Consequently, the burden fell mainly upon the shoulders of the chief clerk, who worked from well before opening time to long after closing time. His superiors ignored his protestations about the need for extra staff; indeed, they regarded them as a sign of weakness on his part. He was utterly exhausted and, sadly, one day he collapsed and died as a result of the strain and worry. Many think that it was because of that regrettable case that CWIP was introduced.

There was much disenchantment generally with the bank in the West Country, and it all came to a head in the famous or perhaps the infamous "Exeter Letter". This was a letter written by a senior manager in the district, and circulated to his colleagues. The result was the nearest thing to a mutiny of the managers ever to be seen in the bank. The letter-writer was immediately suspended. A major enquiry was held at Head Office in Lombard Street and consequently the suspended manager was reinstated, and the local directors of the district were taken to task.

All these matters came to a head in the early 1970s, when I was local head office manager at Chelmsford. Around that time, as well as the introduction of CWIP, we saw the advent of the Industrial Relations Act, and the banks introduced Rate-for-the-Job, which replaced the method of calculating salaries away from the old age-related scheme. Just as all this was happening, Barclays merged with Martins Bank.

The administration problems were legion, but I was very fortunate in Chelmsford district since I had persuaded the local directors to recruit a most able lady from London Eastern district, a Miss Jean Temple. Jean took over responsibility for all the staff grade reassessments, working of course with the local directors. She was one of those persons who could get an immediate grasp of complicated legislation and would come up with the correct ruling in the case of individual staff, every time. Funnily enough, even in the early 1970s, there was a bias against the appointment of women staff in some areas of Barclays Bank, and in other banks too. However, there were other more enlightened senior management who ensured that the brightest women got to senior positions. These positions were more likely to be in administration rather than in front-line banking. Jean had great difficulty in gaining the promotion that she deserved, but eventually her abilities and dedication were rewarded. When she retired she was the business centre manager for the St Ives, Cambridgeshire group of branches. She took this position after being the branch manager of Huntingdon branch, where the then Prime Minister, John Major, held a private account. Jean claims to be the only branch manager to have been kissed by the prime minister! There cannot have been many!

In my day as a branch, or business centre manager, I was often frustrated in my efforts to get promotion for intelligent young women. It was not the bank's management that stopped their progression, but the women themselves. I would plead with them to study and to gain their qualifications through the Institute of Banking examinations, but most would not. So often they had boyfriends, later to become husbands, who were not qualified for anything other than for menial jobs. It seemed that the girls wished to spend all their spare time with them or they did not wish to embarrass their boyfriends by becoming better qualified. By the time that I retired there certainly were far more opportunities for promotion to managerial positions than there ever had been before, and many more women were taking up these situations.

Chapter Six

Cashiering and Relief Work

From 1955 to 1963 I spent time mainly cashiering, but I also had a spell as OC Mech (that was the official title), at 108 High Street branch. During these years I was frequently sent on relief to other branches within the Chelmsford district. I had two more spells at Hadleigh branch as well, but the hardest and most arduous period was from April 1960 to April 1961, when I was working in temporary premises at Basildon, whilst the permanent branch was being built. Basildon was an overspill New Town for the East End of London.

My first proper introduction to cashiering was at 24 High Street, where I was thrown in at the deep end. It was the summer of 1955 when I went on to number five till. This till was situated at the far end of the counter, at the opposite end to the first cashier. The till positions were in order of seniority, and the numbers two, three and four tills, were controlled by much older staff than me. There was a silver-headed lady on the second till, a younger married woman on the third, but on the fourth till there was a man in his fifties, who was not highly rated. He had started banking in the former London and South Western Bank, which had been absorbed into the Barclays group. None of these cashiers wanted to handle the heavy coin credits paid in by Southend Transport. In addition to the Transport, the other cashiers did not want to receive credits from the gas and electricity collectors. All this coin therefore went to number five cashier. Trolley loads of coin would be taken to the strong-room under his supervision. I have described earlier how, as juniors, Don and I had to stack this coin into neat piles. When I was number five cashier, unfortunately, we had only girl juniors, so I had to do the job by myself, or be helped by the messenger if I could find him. The cash was stored under my name until, at the end of the day, what remained would be transferred into the branch reserves. I say "what remained" because there would be a heavy demand for change from the public houses and other amusement arcades and seafront restaurants and the like. When one of the other cashiers received such a demand for full bags of coin, the cashier would take it from my pile, and enter the transaction into the column provided in my till book and indicate which till had taken it. This could happen even when I was away at lunch. Generally, by the end of the day, especially in the summer, my piles of coin would diminish quite rapidly, leaving only a few bags.

After I had been doing the job for a couple of months, Mr Cecil Ling, the manager, later destined to become General Manager, Staff, called me into his office. He was a reserved man who did not often communicate with the staff, especially the more junior members. "I have called you in to compliment you on your performance as a cashier. You have had very few differences. Well done!"

I was amazed. When I returned to my till, the number four cashier asked me why I had been sent for and, rather foolishly, I told him. It may have been a coincidence, but from that day on I would be five or ten pounds short one day and a similar amount over the next. I became embarrassed at having to take the correcting entries to the chief clerk for initialling. Each individual till was sacrosanct in those days. Nobody was allowed to take money from or put money into the till of a cashier, other than the cashier operating that till. The only exception was my coin, stacked in the strong-room. Nowadays there may be three or four people operating the same till, and I do not know how they reconcile responsibility for shortages, or overs. In fact large

45

overs were considered more of a danger than shortages, for it might have meant that a credit slip for a customer had been lost and the account had not been credited. In such cases, cheques could have been returned in error, for lack of funds, which would have been very serious. In my time on the counter the cashier could be in serious trouble for walking away and leaving the till drawer unlocked, for even the shortest of periods. Therefore my main vulnerability was the coin, and the entries in my till book made by other cashiers. Being of a trusting nature, it was not until much later that I wondered whether or not the number four cashier was behind my till differences. He did not have to steal cash, merely to manipulate entries. Whether or not my suspicions were justified I shall never know.

I never really objected to going on relief to other branches. For one thing it meant extra cash in the form of around two shillings and sixpence for lunch allowance, although I believe that with inflation, the amount rose to five shillings before decimalization on 15th February, 1971. The one time that I did object was when I was sent from Hadleigh to another small branch towards the end of December 1954. It was my first experience of balancing the books at the end of the year since I had only returned in July 1954. At our branch, the branch accountant was well organised and we had been made to prepare for the occasion, especially for the ruling-off of our hand-written ledgers and statements. We had worked on this preparation for a week or two leading up to the year-end. I was sent to the other branch because they had staff problems, and even the manager was away sick. This meant that the accountant of that branch had been forced to concentrate on deputising for the manager. This accountant was a rather ineffectual character, and he was certainly not organised. The ordinary staff were left to their own devices, and, consequently nothing had been prepared in advance. The 31st December was a Saturday. We closed at noon, as usual, but with no bank holiday on New Year's Day in those days, we were due to re-open the branch on the Monday morning, having completely finished our balance work on New Year's Eve. On this Saturday, we had to work until eleven p.m., when we had to catch the last bus home.

Few of us had transport other than bicycles in those days, and I was working about fifteen miles from home. The work was far from being finished, and so we had to return on the Sunday morning and it was well past one p.m. before we could go home.

There was no overtime unless the stipulated one hundred and sixty-eight hours had been worked over a four-week period, but the branches were allowed to make a special payment of Balance Money, which was one pound per clerk for June and December and ten shillings for March and September. In the smaller branches, the managers often lived in the bank flat above the branch. At the time this seemed to be a great benefit as the flats were of the highest quality, and were maintained by the bank, with only nominal rents. Sometimes other staff could rent some of the smaller flats that were not wanted by the managers. This all seemed to be quite a perquisite, but later, when home ownership became the norm, many managers found themselves having to leave the flats upon retirement with no equity to put into buying a home.

Reverting to balance days, when the manager of a small branch lived in such a flat, it was almost the expected thing for his wife to appear at teatime with trays of sandwiches, and cakes and cups of tea. All the staff would cease working in order to partake of the meal. Some managers and their wives were very generous and handsome meals were provided. At the half-yearly balance at the end of June, it was not uncommon, especially in country branches, for strawberries and cream to be at the centre of the tea. Essex, especially around Tiptree is renowned for its strawberries, and often the farmer customers would supply the fruit free of charge. These were quite happy occasions.

On another occasion, I was sent to Wickford branch. There the customers were nearly all farmers, and the manager, Mr Deacon, like many other managers in farming communities, was very knowledgeable about farmers and their financial needs, and they respected him highly for it. In ordinary business lending, an overdraft would be marked to be terminated, reviewed or renewed, after a set time limit, such as one month, three months or six months, depending upon the circumstances. Most of the limits marked by Mr Deacon for his farmers were until "Harvest".

Much later in my career when I was Assistant Manager at Stepney Branch, I was sent to act as manager at a small branch on the edge of the London Eastern district, near Barking. The manager was on holiday and the chief clerk was off sick, and I had to step into their shoes completely cold. I loved it!

About the first customer to call was one of the very few farmers who maintained bank accounts in the East End of London. His farm was situated just inside the nearby Essex border, and he was related to a large farming family who were good customers of the Chelmsford district, and his name was familiar to me. He called to complain that London Eastern Local Head Office was harassing him. He had taken up the offer of a grant from the Ministry of Agriculture and Fisheries in order to build a milking parlour for his newly acquired herd, following his transferring from arable to dairy farming. The ministry was encouraging such transfers of land use in those days. He had needed some cash from the bank to supplement his working capital, and the bank had agreed to grant an overdraft. He had not exceeded his limits and was a responsible and conscientious borrower.

"They want to take away my overdraft," he complained. "The arrangement was for me to repay the overdraft from my milk cheque from the Milk Marketing Board, but my heifers are still in calf!"

It took some doing, but I did eventually get the Assistant District Manager for the section to agree to an extension. This goes to show how vital it is for a lender to understand the trade of his customer. I have heard of many similar examples of managers being appointed to areas where they do not know the indigenous trade. In some cases it can be much to their disadvantage when crafty locals catch on to the flaws of a manager's knowledge of the trade, be it fishing, weaving, mining etc.

Around 1956 there was a tragedy at our branch on Canvey Island. One morning Mrs Souster found the manager, Mr Souster, dead in his bed. The couple lived in the bank flat above the branch. It was a comfortable life, and, as I was told the story, Mrs Souster would often take her husband his breakfast on a tray in bed. He would then get up at about eight a.m. and prepare himself for a day in the office. It was thus that Mrs Souster discovered that he had suffered a heart attack and died whilst she was downstairs getting his breakfast. As a result, there was much confusion at the branch when the staff arrived. It was not a large branch, perhaps eight members of staff, with an accountant as deputy to the manager. The poor accountant had many tasks upon his plate. As well as organising the branch, he had to help to console Mrs Souster, and to help her organise her day. Her son, David, also worked in the bank, but not at Canvey. He and I were to work side by side a couple of years later. David who had already left for work had to return home to comfort his mother and to help organise all the necessary arrangements following the death of his father.

I was on the counter at 24 High Street when I was summoned to make my way to Canvey branch to work as a relief cashier. The branch opened at normal time, ten a.m. I arrived shortly after to find the banking hall full of locals who, having just heard the news, were calling to express their condolences. It was a tight-knit community, and Mr Souster had been highly respected on the island. As I started to prepare to work, taking over the till keys and checking the contents of the padlocked black, round till-can that cash from the tills were stored in when placed in the strong-room overnight, I started chatting to another member of the staff. The subject of age came up. "When is your birthday?" I was asked. I gave the information just as I was altering the date on my cashier's date stamp used for cancelling cheques, receipting paying-in books and so on. With my mind not on what I was doing, instead of putting in the correct date, I had inserted my birthday date into my rubber stamp. That day all the work that I processed was shown to be on a date some four months later! I did not discover my error until I was altering the date on the stamp next morning. I remained on relief at the branch until after the funeral, but the matter was never raised. What confusion my stupid error might have caused later, when people were trying to reconcile their cheques and paying-in slips to their bank statements, I shall never know, maybe no one ever noticed. I hope not.

Canvey Island branch had suffered from the terrible floods of February 1953, when the whole island had been cut off by floods whipped-up by storm force north-easterly winds. The sea wall had been breached and like many houses the bank branch had been flooded up to almost first floor level. People in bungalows had been forced to climb on to their roofs in the middle of the bitterly cold night to await rescue, and many lives were lost. Canvey is only just an "island", since it is linked to the mainland by a road bridge of about fifty yards in length. It is extremely flat, and many of the roads are named after the Dutchmen who reclaimed the land many years ago.

When the floods came, the branch records were all immersed in muddy seawater. After the floods had receded, and the dirty water had been pumped out of the basement, teams of inspectors had to help dry all the ledgers and securities sheets (where customers' items lodged for safe-keeping or deposited were recorded). All records were recorded in pen and ink, using the bank's specially approved ink, except for some where some clerks had used the then new biro ball-tipped pens, the use of which had been forbidden by the chief inspector. All the hand-written sheets were hung out on clotheslines to dry like washing. In the end, the only writing that remained legible was that which had been written with the biros, and from then on biros were permitted in the bank. How the staff managed to reconstruct all the other bank and customer records I do not know. I think that the bank must have needed to rely heavily upon the trustworthiness and co-operation of its branch customers.

My worst experience of cashiering was in temporary premises in the early days of the construction of the Town Centre of Basildon in 1960. The branch was originally opened in 1959 as a sub-branch to Laindon, Essex, about two miles away. The prefabricated wooden building stood upon open land next to the newly erected bus station, and next to a similar hut erected for the branch of Westminster Bank. This was before that bank merged with National

Provincial Bank. NP, as it was known, had its branch in one of the few brick-built newly constructed offices in East Walk. Barclays' new building in East Walk was just a hole in the ground, which had to be frequently pumped out because of the very wet spring and summer of that year. Our hut was built to accommodate about six to eight staff, but by the time that we were ready to move into the new building the numbers had risen to about eighteen. There was no place to work, especially when the cashier who ran the sub-branch at Nevendon, also a wooden hut, returned to the branch in the late afternoon.

When I had joined the branch in April 1960, there were about eight staff. The branch had been upgraded to a full branch, and the manager of Laindon branch, Mr Stuart Barker, moved down to run the New Town branch, leaving a Mr Andrews as manager of Laindon. The staff of Basildon was comprised of the manager, his secretary, the accountant, myself as cashier, a woman Adler statement machine operator, a ledger-poster, a junior and the sub-branch cashier. The counter had only two positions, and the second was for the Adler operator, who was expected to help when there was a queue of customers, if she was able to get away from her statement posting.

Basildon was beginning to grow rapidly as new shops and stores opened. Furniture stores did very well with all the new residents arriving mostly from the East End of London. They were buying new furniture on the easy-to-pay-back hire purchase schemes, which had only recently become available to most working-class people. There was no railway station, which was a deliberate part of the planning by the New Town Commission, in order to prevent it being turned into a commuter town. The Commission wanted all the workers to be employed in the newly constructed industrial areas on the other side of the town They did not want the new residents to go back to working in London as this would defeat the purpose of the new town. Besides furniture shops there came the supermarkets. There were few corner shops, except in some of the outlying residential areas. One of the busiest supermarkets, until bigger opposition was to arrive later was Victor Value, situated close to the other side of

51

the bus station. In addition to Victor Value, there was the local Co-op. Both these stores plus Littlewoods, the first department store to open in Basildon, banked with or through our branch, as did the Basildon Development Corporation and Basildon Council. All the credits for the stores were paid in to us, but the accounts were mainly domiciled in London or other large towns.

The daily cash intake was very substantial, and at the weekends there were wages to pay. Much of the cash needed to pay the factories was taken by the Nevendon sub-branch cashier in a taxi. We used one taxi driver on a regular basis. Terry Dove, the ex-Arsenal goalkeeper, was a fit giant of a man, and was reliable and very trustworthy and he later became a town councillor.

Each morning my first job was to pay the clearing. Then I had to empty the night safe of the wallets, which had been deposited the night before. There would be about thirty of these each morning, but on Monday mornings there could be about fifty, and we had to have a larger safe installed to accommodate them all. Black wallets could be opened by the branch, and the brown wallets were for customers to collect and to open themselves before paying in the contents. The majority was black and it created quite a task to open them, pull out the rolled-up contents, count the notes (no coin would be enclosed) and sort out the cheques. If there were any errors the customers had to be advised before the credit could be processed, and these errors were frequent. It was usually impossible to clear all the black wallets before opening time, when I had to attend to all the customers coming through the door. Many would be collecting their brown wallets and paying in the contents. In those pre-decimalization days, the notes were mainly of one-pound or ten-shilling denominations. The old white five-pound notes had been withdrawn, although a few showed up now and again, and were sent to Bank of England for collection. If proved genuine, the Bank of England would send a credit to the customer's account. The new blue five-pound notes were in circulation, but were mainly used in larger transactions. It would not have been a wise thing to offer one to a bus conductor for a threepenny fare! On a Monday, especially, I would have to make up HVPs to the value of around £50,000, which was a lot of money in those days. We would have to take them in the manager's, or more usually, in the accountant's car to the main post office in Laindon. The accountant's car was a very old Austin, which could just about manage to struggle the two miles to the post office, bearing its load of the two of us, both quite large men, plus the parcels. On at least one occasion it gave up the ghost, and we had to telephone for assistance whilst we waited by the roadside with a fortune in parcels on the back seat.

Checking the bundles of one hundred pounds of one-pound notes or of fifty pounds of ten-shilling notes was irksome. I was not keen on a couple of Smart Alec types who paid in from Victor Value. They would bring in huge credits made up of bundles of one-pound and ten-shilling notes, for which, when I was busy, as I usually was, I would give a "bulk" receipt, on the understanding that I would count the notes later. This was usual practice for the larger account customers such as the Co-op or the Basildon Council Rent Collection Department. Once all the cash was agreed, a proper receipt would be given. Victor Value's notes were usually scruffy and often sticky and had to be sorted so that they were not re-issued but sent to the Bank of England to be destroyed. Counting them was a nightmare, especially under pressure. Nearly every bundle would be wrong, usually with too many notes in a bundle. Every time a bundle was found to be wrong, it had to be recounted. This took up much valuable time. If it was over, the notes would be taken out and returned to the customer, or the customer would be contacted and might agree to the value of the paying-in slip being increased. If the bundle was short another member of staff had to double-check it. A new band would replace the original paper band (blue for one-pound and orange for ten-shilling notes) and the old one returned to the customer as evidence. On one memorable occasion, I walked round to Victor Value with some blue bands. I pointed out the ones where there were shortages, and which had been double-checked. We then went through the ones where I had found surpluses. I gave them back the notes, less those that had replaced the shortages and showed them the bands of the bundles in surplus. Imagine my surprise when the young man gave a hoot of joy, "Got you! " he exclaimed. "That bundle was three pounds over not two! See, here is my mark. You have kept the third!" I was incensed at this accusation of dishonesty, when what mainly concerned me was their incompetence. I made him return to the branch with me, and in front of the manager I recounted the bundle, which was, as he claimed, one pound over. The notes were in a sticky mess and two notes were virtually stuck together. Instead of being satisfied, he turned upon me.

"Well, if I had not had told you, you would have come back and taken the note out of the packet!" A pound was quite a lot of money in those days, and I could well have done with a few more in my wage packet, but I was not a thief. But what was so infuriating was to think that despite all the work that went into getting this man's work right for him, he was setting traps to ensnare me, and was deliberately causing us problems with bundles containing the wrong amount of cash. Fortunately our manager complained to the head office of Victor Value, and the man shortly disappeared from the scene.

Basildon contained many honest and hard-working new citizens, but, according to the local police, many rogues, burglars, shoplifters and the like had also come into the town from the East End. They told how, on one residential building site, where new methods were being used, the roof covering about six terraced houses was in one long prefabricated strip which was supposed to be bolted down. The police reckoned that the men building this terrace had deliberately left the roof insecurely bolted at the ends so that they could gain entrance by this route at a later date. The time was just before the Great Train Robbery, but if these "villains", as they were known to the local police, had known about the value of our HVPs being taken to Laindon Post Office in that dilapidated old Austin, I would not have given much for our chances.

On occasions I would change places with Tony Grew, who was the sub-branch cashier. As I have said, this sub-branch was also a wooden hut, with only a toilet and a two-man counter. Like the main branch, it was gas lit, with only gas mantles for lighting. A dear old chap, of about seventy-two, who was his "guard", would accompany the cashier. Actually, I think that he was more of a guard on behalf of the bank and was there to see that the cashier did not abscond with the funds! I did not consider him to be much of a guard for the cashier as he was far too frail. There was one benefit from going to the sub-branch – the cashier was paid lunch money. A cheap, hot meal was also available by arrangement with the staff canteen of a nearby customer company known as Ships' Carbon Limited. The guard would collect this meal at midday on a tray. The trouble was then in trying to eat it whilst serving customers. Of course, when the guard had gone to collect the meal, the cashier was left alone. I think that the bank inspectors would have disapproved of this arrangement, had they visited the sub-branch at the wrong time. Back at the main branch, I would usually eat sandwiches at my till, not having time to take a lunch-break.

One day, Terry Dove picked me up in his taxi, with my bag containing cash chained to my arm, and drove me and the guard the two and a half miles approximately to the sub-branch. On our way there, a workman's van drove out of a side road and collided with us. Terry sprung into action. He thought that it was part of a scheme to rob us. He ran to the van door and dragged the poor protesting driver out of his van and pinioned him. Eventually, when he was satisfied that it was not a hold up, he let him go. The damage to the taxi was slight, and so we drove on to the sub-branch.

On another occasion, the local chief inspector of police had been tipped off that there was to be a raid on the sub-branch. I had the misfortune to be in charge on the day in question. The chief inspector was excited in anticipation of catching his villains. Two of his officers lay in wait in the toilet ready to spring out at a given signal. He had other policemen posted near at hand, whilst he tried to make himself as inconspicuous as possible behind the door leading to the counter. As the day wore on and it got closer to the time for us to close the sub-branch and to return to the main branch, we could sense his disappointment that the villains had not shown themselves. Of course, there was the possibility that they were going to come at the last moment! This served to heighten the tension and excitement, but nothing happened. Perhaps the villains had also received a tip-off – who knows? It was a bitterly disappointed chief inspector, but also a much-relieved cashier who locked up the sub-branch at two-thirty p.m. The police escorted us back to the main office, where we waved them a fond farewell.

Chapter Seven

Odds and Ends
and Personal Loans

Before I pass on to my management days, there are a few sundry matters that I hope the reader will find to be of interest. Unfortunately, they do not really fit under any other heading.

During my seven years in the navy, I served in my first ship, a Battle Class destroyer, HMS *Aisne*. The boatswain of this ship was a very capable and much-liked seaman petty officer, Frank Boxall. He was a tough chap of about forty, who could handle himself well. The officers respected him, and so did the men under him. As boatswain he would attend the gathering of all the seamen on watch on the quarter-deck, when hands fell in at eight a.m. Under the eye of the officer-of-the-day, or, sometimes, the first lieutenant, he would detail off working parties for the forenoon watch. Some would be sent to paint various areas of the ship, others would form a working party to attend to the ship's boats, and other jobs – perhaps cleaning the heads, or the ship's passages – would be handed to others. On other occasions when he was duty petty officer, he would accompany the officer-of-the-day when the latter carried out evening rounds after "Hands to tea and shift into night clothing" had been piped. This was an inspection of the messes to see that they were tidy, and that all hands who were not on watch had changed out of their working clothes into the rig to be worn on board during the evening.

I was a junior storekeeper and, one evening, I had been working, busily cleaning and tidying a storeroom immediately below my own mess. Access to this storeroom was through a hatch resembling a manhole cover in the deck of the mess. I had just emerged and battened down the hatch cover, when the officer-of-the-day accompanied by Frank Boxall arrived on the mess-deck. "Put that man on a charge, Petty Officer," instructed the lieutenant to Frank. The officer had not waited for any explanations, nor had he wanted any! It was therefore for the one and only time in my seven years' service that, next morning, I had approached the captain's table for "defaulters". I dutifully removed my cap, as was the routine for defaulters, and was charged with being out of the rig-of-the-day at evening rounds. Fortunately, my own stores petty officer appeared to give evidence that I had been working under his orders, and the case was grudgingly dismissed. From then on I never emerged from a storeroom until after the evening rounds had finished.

I tell this story because about six years later when I returned to the bank, who should I find as bank messenger to 108 High Street branch? None other than Frank Boxall! I had always known that he was my "Towny", as people from the same town were known in the navy, but I had little anticipated that we would ever meet again, once I had left the ship. We worked in the same branch for a couple of years when I was both OC Mech and a cashier.

Oddly enough, the chap who took over my OC Mech duties, John Harker, had just returned from National Service having also served in HMS *Aisne*. He had joined her a couple of months after I had left, but since he was an Ordinary Seaman, Frank had been his boss. We had many a laugh over this reversal of roles. Frank was very hard-working in the mornings, since he and his wife, jointly, had the contract to clean the branch, and they would do this before the staff arrived each morning. In the afternoon, however, we could seldom find him, and we believed him to be out delivering his messages. Later we discovered that he used to go round collecting bets for a local bookmaker for a couple of hours each day, whilst the racing was on!

At 108 High Street branch, the machine-room was above the counter. The method of passing requests for statements, or any other documents or papers to the machine-room was by means of a metal chute. A length of string to which was tied a large bulldog clip dangled down the chute from the machine-room above. The items or messages to be sent to the machine-room staff would be attached to the bulldog clip. The cashier would rap on the metal chute, and the upstairs staff would haul up the string and remove the content from the clip, and then drop the clip back. Any statements or other items to be handed to the customers would be delivered down the chute in like fashion. It sounds crude but it worked. It was a far more efficient method, however, than the expensive but painfully slow electrically operated book lifts that were built into new offices.

It was whilst I was working as a cashier in 108 High Street, that the Bank of England changed the packaging of surplus notes, or notes for destruction. Previously, we had wrapped them, as I have described earlier in the book, in strong brown paper packages and tied them with string, and then sealed them over the knot in the string. This was very time-consuming, and it was not possible to see the contents of the packages until they were opened. There were rumours that, despite the rule that there had to be two signatures on each package, i.e. that of the person making up the package and that of the checker, some packages, upon being opened, had been found to contain newspaper cut down to the size of bank notes! Often in such a case, the checker had been guilty of signing a package, which he or she had not seen being made up. With the increased introduction of polythene into everyday life, the Bank of England agreed to have notes placed into transparent polythene packets, which were then hermetically sealed. This was a great improvement, but one day I nearly made a serious error. I was making up a wages order to be collected by a company. The companies would send lists to the branch, probably on the previous day, showing the desired breakdown of notes and coin required to make up the entire individual wage packets for the workers. The Truck Acts were still in force, and it was legally binding that all workers should receive their wages in cash only. It was the practice to make up these wage lists well in advance of the customer calling, perhaps on the evening preceding the day of collection. The notes and coin would be counted, prepared, checked by a second cashier and placed in a bag to be sealed under the signature of the two cashiers involved in the preparation.

On this occasion, I almost put in bundles of blue five-pound notes, which were slightly larger than the green one-pound notes, which I had intended to pack. It would not have mattered because the cash going into the bag would have been checked by my colleague, and I am sure that the mistake would have been noticed then or when had I balanced my till, that evening. What occurred to me was that, when serving on the counter and passing large values of cash to a customer when under pressure, such a mistake made on the spur of the moment could be very costly, especially if the customer was tempted to keep the overpayment. The persons collecting the cash were often only employees of the company, and probably on low wages, and, although nearly all were known to us and were very honest, someone might have yielded to temptation.

As a result of this experience, I sent off my recommendation to the Ideas Committee for the packages to be of coloured polythene, although still to remain transparent. I suggested a pale but different colour be applied to each of the denominations. The Ideas Committee was made up of representatives of the staff as well as members from the bank management. They made cash awards for successful suggestions. I waited a long time before, hearing nothing, I telephoned the secretary of the committee who said that the idea had been put forward to Head Office Inspection Department for consideration. She said that she would follow up to see why I had heard nothing. Shortly after, I received a phone call from a lady, presumably a secretary from Inspection Department. She sounded rather harassed, and her attitude implied that she was not very pleased with me. "If you only knew what trouble we had to get the Bank of England to accept our original proposals for a suitable packet! And we have had to place an order for thousands of the present-style packets."

It was obvious that she would have liked me to drop the matter, but I dug in my toes. Eventually the new coloured packets were introduced and have been in use by all the banks ever since. I received my due award for a suggestion that may well have saved the bank thousands of pounds in cash losses. It was the princely sum of two guineas. During the course of my career I received four awards for ideas to help the bank. I think the largest was for ten guineas, which I shared with a branch colleague, with whom I had collaborated in solving a problem. That was in the 1960s, and the increase was due only to inflation. Later, in the 1980s, the bank began to be more generous for rewarding suggestions, which led to improvements, especially those which directly cut costs.

In the early 1960s I had nearly completed my banking examinations, but not only because of working lengthy hours but also having two young children at home, I was struggling with the final subject, The Practice of Banking. I had returned for a third time to Hadleigh, Essex branch, which had grown considerably from the days of my first two spells there. The second-in-command was no longer an accountant, but my friend Bruce Jeffreys, who had been appointed chief clerk. Bruce was one of the two juniors immediately before Don Miller and I, who went into National Service from 24 High Street branch in 1945. The branch was no longer on hand-posting and waste, but was fully mechanised. The staff had increased to about ten, and I was made securities clerk, and deputised for Bruce in his absence. I was now keen to get promotion myself, but I first needed to go on a Stage II course, which was reserved for recognised securities clerks who had obtained their AIB.

There were able men being promoted who had not passed any examinations, and one of these was Don Miller. At that time he had just been made chief clerk of 24 High Street branch. First, however, he had been an instructor on the Stage II securities course. It was through him that I had discovered that it was *not* essential to have attained the AIB in order to *instruct* upon this course. Normally only those with their AIB could go on the course, unless there were very extenuating circumstances or if they had been nominated to instruct on the course. I therefore tried the ploy by requesting to be made a course instructor, and to my surprise I was accepted. First, I had to go on the course, which I did in April 1963, just after making another attempt to pass The Practice of Banking exam. Whilst on the course two or three of the class received notices from their districts offering them promotion to chief clerk, once the course had been completed. The course went well for me, and to my delight, shortly after returning to the branch I had received notification that I had been successful with the Practice of Banking, and I obtained my AIB. A month later, in July 1963, I was promoted to chief clerk of Rochford, Essex branch and I was never called back to the bank training centre at Wimbledon as an instructor for the Stage II course.

Eighteen months later, on 2nd January 1965, I was appointed Assistant Manager, at the 45 Victoria Avenue, Southend branch, which had been opened in 1963. In spite of some resistance, the bank had endeavoured to persuade some customers to move, and in some cases had shanghaied some customers' accounts from the old branches at 24 and 108 High Street to this new branch, situated in the rapidly expanding new business area of Victoria Avenue. This avenue had been the residential area for the better-off citizens of the borough, but now the large Victorian houses were being demolished at a breath-taking pace and were being replaced by tall office blocks. It was a developers' paradise.

The first inkling that I had that I might be given the post of Assistant Manager had come from Reg Wilshire, one of the messengers at 45 Victoria Avenue. I had gone to 45 Victoria Avenue branch to collect some banknotes for Rochford branch, and as I stood at the counter, Reg called out, "You know that you will be taking over from Phil Cole, when he becomes a full manager!" I did not know, and neither, it was obvious, did any others of the staff at 45 Victoria Avenue. It was out of the question since I had been a chief clerk for only just over a year. Since coming back to the bank I was to come to realise that very few of my contemporaries had equipped themselves for managerial promotion despite the seven-year start that I had given them. I had achieved a chief clerkship only nine years after really setting out on a banking career, and such promotion was very unusual in those days. It had taken Don Miller, one of the really bright rising stars, thirteen years to get to chief clerk, although he might have got there earlier if he had obtained his AIB. There were many other worthier and more deserving contenders for the job of assistant manager of 45 Victoria Avenue than me. However, as in the Royal Navy, where the destinations of most ships in the fleet are not known to their crews, the Dockyard Mateys (dockyard workers) always know, and so it was with the bank messengers. There was not much that they did not know about well in advance and it appeared that there was some weird but mainly reliable grapevine that circulated amongst them.

When my appointment did come through, I was certainly not the only one to be surprised. Many people were quite offended, especially those who had considered themselves to be better entitled to the job, and who probably had a case. Many thought that Don Miller should have had the appointment, and I would have agreed with them. One frustrated contemporary, a year or two older than me, complained to Local Head Office. He was summoned to see the local directors, and was rebuked for having the audacity to have questioned their judgement. I was very pleased with the appointment, but wished that it had come in a different way and had not caused so much bad feeling. I held no sway with the local directors, and I did not have influential relatives who, in some districts, might have helped many a less competent clerk to obtain a position in the old days, if only one of relatively minor status. Alan Smith, my manager at Rochford, who at age forty-two was quite a young manager, was genuinely pleased for me. "Assistant manager at thirty-five! You will be a general manager within ten years!" – A prediction that was not to come true.

Before all this happened, and whilst I was cashier at Basildon, the economic climate had changed. Just as Harold Macmillan had commented upon the "Wind of Change" running though South Africa upon the occasion of his visit to that unhappy nation, the first real economic recovery following the end of the Second World War was burgeoning. Mr Macmillan had been able to tell us, "You have never had it so good!" and we were able believe him. I have already mentioned that the families arriving as new residents in the New Town were discarding their old furniture and furnishing their new rented homes with items acquired on hire purchase. Credit was becoming very freely obtainable, although this was some six years before the advent of the Barclaycard, which was the first, and for some time the *only* credit card in the UK. The banks wished to get in on this new and profitable credit boom.

I remember that one Tuesday in August 1958 it was announced on the BBC news programmes that the Midland Bank was going to introduce Personal Instalment Loans (Glossary 10), from the Monday of the following week. Typically, Barclays, not to be outdone and wishing to maintain its position as the number one bank in Britain, announced that it would introduce these loans with immediate effect! The staff had no idea what a Personal Loan (as they were generally known) was! This shortfall in their knowledge was to be quickly repaired as the demand for such loans took off very rapidly. These unsecured loans of up to £500 initially enabled the borrowers to take cash to purchase new furniture or even new cars, and having cash often enabled them to get generous discounts. To get such a loan, the borrower, who might not previously have been a bank customer, merely had to obtain a bank reference, usually from a friend who had a bank account; open a current account and then give some evidence of income. In my position as cashier at Basildon, I would often see new customers go into the manager's room and then emerge with a new chequebook. With the manager's agreement, they would withdraw up to five hundred pounds in cash, and it was seldom less than five hundred pounds!

One man and his wife bought a large Vauxhall Estate, and after a few days they and their three young children were found to have given up their home and were *living in this car*. Of course, the authorities had to get them re-housed, but I cannot remember if they repaid their loan.

The Personal loan carried its own life insurance, so that it was eliminated on the death of a borrower. I suppose that Head Office actually wrote-off the loan, but it would be shown as having been repaid in the branch's records. This was just as well for, on one of the very first loans that our manager, Stuart Barker, granted, a borrower bought a large car, and, the very next day, he and his companion, whom I believe was his wife, set off on a long journey to the north of the country. On the way they had to stop behind a tipper-lorry which was full of sand. For whatever reason, the tipper started to rise up and the whole load of sand covered our customer's car, and the occupants were suffocated.

On the more humorous side, I recall that the Tilbury branch of one of the main clearing banks quickly developed a problem. As I have said, because of the provisions of the Truck Acts, most workers were paid in cash and few had bank accounts. The advent of the Personal Loan Scheme helped to persuade more workers to open bank accounts. The loan would be paid into the current account and drawn off as and when needed, which was usually the full amount on the first day. The customer was then obliged to feed cash into the account to meet the monthly repayment programme.

It so happened that at this Tilbury branch of X Bank, one of their docker customers had a long-standing current account, and one day he called to take out a personal loan. He found it pretty easy to get this money and must have told his friends. Over the next couple of weeks he gave references for a number of his friends who wanted to open current accounts. In those days, wise bank managers insisted on at least two references, one of which should be the employer, especially where the employer was a large and well-respected organisation. Other managers, and, indeed, their superiors were beginning to feel the competition and were satisfied to take one reference from a person already holding a bank account, since that person must have been recommended in the first place. The real reason for taking a reference was to prove the identity of the applicant, not his honesty. The bank could have been accused of conversion if it were to have placed funds by way of cheques to the account of a person who was not who he or she purported to be.

The manager of X Bank branch was well pleased with all the accounts he was gaining through the introductions of his old customer, and the pace began to quicken when the new customers also began to make introductions. Nearly every new customer wanted a personal loan. For about six months all was well, and then things started to deteriorate. Repayments on the personal loans, which were usually spread over twelve to twenty-four months, began to dry up. The borrowing customers could not be traced at the addresses that they had given, and only then did the penny drop! When the new customers had taken their loans, they had not withdrawn the whole sum but had left sufficient cash in the current account to repay the first six monthly instalments. As everything had been flowing smoothly, the branch had not needed to contact any of its new customers until the current account funds had begun to run out. The branch then realised that the loans were being repaid with the bank's own money! The losses were reported to be around ten thousand pounds which does not seem much these days, but it was a fortune in the days when a brand new Austin Mini or Volkswagen Beetle could be bought for only a fraction over five hundred pounds.

When I was at Stepney branch, some six years later, I served under a renowned and revered banker, Mr Joe Holmes. He was one of the old characters whose names were legend. He would not grant, nor would he allow any of his staff to grant personal loans. He ignored the protestations of the local directors, who were being pressurised by Head Office to push this innovation in an attempt to increase the market-share of worker and lower middle-class customers. One day one of the assistant general managers who himself had once managed Stepney Branch telephoned him. "Joe," he had asked, "why are you disobeying instructions and not granting personal loans? Yours is the only branch in the country with a nil return."

"Because I am a banker," replied Joe, "and personal loans are not banking." He never did give way, but some personal loans were eventually granted by his subordinates, but only to established customers whose integrity was beyond doubt. The irony was that the major furniture store in Basildon to profit most from the personal loan boom was Killwicks, a customer of Stepney.

The most humorous story of all that I know concerning personal loans, involved a man called K, who had obtained personal loans from every one of the six banks in Basildon. These banks were Barclays, Westminster, Midland, Lloyds, National Provincial and Williams & Glyn. None of the repayments were being maintained, so debt collectors were used, and then Mr K agreed to pay in regularly – but these payments were not enough to cover even the interest on his loan. He would pay in a derisory six pounds per week to Williams & Glyn Bank, whose manager would laboriously make out five credit slips, each for one pound and distribute them around the other banks in the town. I am sure that this exercise was far from cost-effective. For how long he kept up this weekly charade I cannot remember, but in the end the whole of the remaining outstanding debts at all the banks had to be written off. That, however, is not the end of the story.

One busy Monday afternoon, I was working hard to clear and balance my till, when I realised that somebody was knocking at our window. Being only a temporary building in a wooden hut, it did not have a knocker or a bell. I made the usual gestures to show that we were closed, but the party, a man and his wife and two young children, would not accept "No" for an answer, and continued to rap on the window. Eventually our chief clerk, who had been made up from accountant as a result of the increase in staff, said that we had better let them in. He was a kindly man, and realised that as our building was right beside the bus station they had probably come some way on the bus, and he was right. In the absence of the manager, the chief clerk asked them what they wanted, and they replied that within a few days they would be moving to Basildon and they wanted to buy furniture for their new home. They did not have a bank account, but would like to open one. This meant that they needed the two references, which we insisted upon. Names and addresses were given and then they asked if, once the account was open, they could have a personal loan to buy their furniture. The chief clerk started to fill in the signature card, which was required upon opening an account. "What are your names, please?" asked the chief clerk. "Mr and Mrs K," had come the answer. The chief clerk looked at them quizzically, but before he could ask any questions, the man had jumped in with a smile upon his face, "I think you know my brother. He is a bad lot! He owes money everywhere, and has done so all his life. He is, I am afraid, the proverbial black sheep of our family. As you can see, we are different. I have brought along my wife and family to prove to you that we are a happy and hard-working family. I am in regular employment as a bus driver with London Transport. The Eastern National Bus Company have offered me a job after we move to Basildon."

Although the chief clerk felt a little uneasy, he realised how wrong it was to consider that, because one apple was rotten, all the rest in the barrel had to be rotten too. Therefore he told them that they could call for their personal loan the following week provided that all the references were in order. Some of us advised him to think again. "What if it did go wrong, especially knowing about the brother? The branch would have a lot of egg on its face!"

He laughed it off. "You are all too pessimistic! Here is a chance to do business with a decent family. We should not turn it down because of the brother's reputation." Well, as you will have guessed, he lent the money, but he never saw a penny paid back.

Life in small country branches was very relaxed and friendly, as I was to find out whilst chief clerk at Rochford. Although only just outside the Borough of Southend-on-Sea, it was a very separate entity, and very proud of its history. Rochford Town Square, where our branch was sited, was reputedly the last place in England where witches had been burned at the stake. Rochford and its surrounding area housed some very wealthy and influential landowners. The Lord-Lieutenant of the County was a customer. At one time, Rochford was the major town in the area, and the first banking branch in Southend-on-Sea was opened as a sub-branch to Rochford. I found some old journals in the vaults of the branch that contained daily records. Amongst many interesting items were the accounts kept of the sub-branch clerk who travelled to and from Southend by pony-and-trap, and took his dog with him. He was given a small stipend to cover his expenses.

The bank staff in rural areas would often go the extra mile to help their customers in many ways. At Rochford we had one poor old lady who was bedridden, and lived just about one hundred and fifty yards from the office. She would send a child with a message asking for cash or for some other service. I would take one of the clerks around to her terraced cottage, which had a front door going straight into the front parlour from the street. She had shifted her bed into this parlour. The front door would be closed but not locked. I would knock. "Come in!" she would call out, and we would enter, as would all her other tradesmen when they delivered her groceries, meat, milk and so on. The insurance man and the rent collector would do the same. I would hand her the cash required in exchange for a cheque, or get a receipt for any other item that I had delivered. She was not poor, and was quite intelligent, but suffered badly from arthritis.

One of my jobs was to sign any letters that I had dictated myself, which were mainly internal or administrative, but I had always to scrutinise all carbon copies of letters leaving the branch, including those signed by the manager. This was usually a formality, but occasionally something would be spotted and, one hoped, corrected before the junior took the letters to post. On one memorable occasion, our manager's secretary, who was first-class and who was later to become a local director's secretary, made a magnificent bloomer, which the manager had not spotted, and which I very nearly missed. Coming to the valediction of a letter to a very wealthy and highly respected local landowner and gentleman farmer, the letter concluded: "...and I hope that both you and Mrs X are peeing well"! A mis-type for "keeping well". Fortunately the letter was rescued and re-typed before leaving the office.

In the country branches, bank staff, especially the managers and their seconds-in-command, and some cashiers would be given bags of potatoes or such-like by the farmers. A turkey for Christmas was quite the norm for the manager. The trouble was that one could never be quite sure that it was coming. The farmer would usually deliver it late on Christmas Eve. Not daring to risk not having a bird for the family, the manager's wife would purchase one from the butcher, only to end up with two.

There was a renowned butcher's shop in the centre of Rochford. The butcher would slaughter all his own meat in the little barn-type annex, where he would often keep his victims overnight before slaughtering them. It was pitiful to hear them lowing before they were killed. On one occasion, the butcher, as was his wont, had attended the local agricultural show and purchased the prize bullock. The next day his counter was decked with the rosettes, which covered cuts and joints of meat. One knowledgeable lady, the wife of a local smallholder, came into the shop and in front of all the other customers told the butcher to remove all the rosettes. "That is not the prize bullock, Mr H," she complained. "That bullock is still alive in your slaughter house!" As if to endorse her words, a long, tremulous "Moo-oo" emitted from the building! The embarrassed Mr H had been rumbled!

I had really enjoyed my eighteen months in Rochford. I had arrived a stranger, but had departed as a fully paid-up member of the community! It was not entirely a smooth ride in my first appointment. On the first occasion that I was left in charge of the branch, not long after my arrival, I was called upon to arrange my first loan to a customer, without having a manager on hand to consult. I think the customer sensed that I was new to lending, because I made such a meal of lending about five hundred pounds that in the end he wisely said that he would leave it until the manager returned. I felt rather chastened by this but in some ways I was relieved.

The career profile in those days was somewhat ambiguous. To reach a manager's chair it was necessary to prove to be a good securities clerk, which meant being academically sound. From securities clerk the next step was to be a chief clerk, which was a job for an administrator and for a person having a talent in man-management. There were no courses then available that taught either administration/staff-management, or lending. These abilities had to be natural, or picked up along the way. Consequently, many a good securities clerk, who could have made a good lending manager even though no good at administration or staff control, failed as a chief clerk, and progressed no further or was demoted. On the other hand, good chief clerks often failed as lending managers. It was often said that one never knew a person's capability until that person had been over-promoted.

Among our business customers at Basildon, we had a young barrow-boy type who was buying up meat and poultry at wholesale prices from Smithfields, the London meat market, and selling it on cheaply. My part-time second cashier, a pretty woman, once asked him if he had any chickens for sale. Chicken was not the common everyday meal in those days, and it was still regarded as a luxury meal by most people. He said that he would let her have one for a pound, which was very cheap for a plump bird. As a result, the rest of the staff asked if they too could buy chickens at that price. The outcome was that, nearly every Friday from then on, he would arrive in his van and distribute around half-a-dozen chickens to the staff at a pound a time. We had wondered how he could do it, and the answer was that he could not. It turned out that, in order to keep his cash flow going, he was selling his meat and poultry for less than he was paying for it, with bankruptcy being the inevitable conclusion. We all felt a sense of guilt, feeling that we had contributed to his downfall, but our contribution had been only a drop in the ocean of his overall problem. The trouble was that he had left the bank with an overdraft that had to be written off, and this had added to our sense of guilt!

Before I leave Basildon as it was, in the wooden hut, there is other amusing detail. We may not have had a doorbell, but we did have an alarm bell. The branch was not connected to the police station, as most are in modern times, and we had to rely upon the sound of the alarm bell to attract the police, or some public-minded citizen in case of a raid or a burglary. Our cleaner, a dear little old lady, would clean the branch starting at six-thirty a.m. every morning and she would usually have departed by the time the staff arrived. I was usually the first, and would drive up to the branch and, before parking it for the day, put my battered old motor cycle and sidecar unit outside the front door whilst I opened up the branch. Nearly every morning without fail, as I switched off the engine, I would hear the alarm bell ringing at full blast. The cleaner had been shown countless times how to deactivate the alarm before entering but she seldom managed to do it. The alarm would be ringing for about two hours until I arrived to turn it off, and nobody would ever take any notice of it. It is a wonder that the local police chief inspector's "villains" had not found out how vulnerable the branch was, first thing in the morning!

I was at Basildon for one week in the new town centre building, which seemed huge when it opened in April 1961. In less than ten years it had to be extended by taking in the first floor restaurant, which was running at a loss anyway. On the first opening of the premises in 1961, the chief clerk was detailed to show parties of guests around the new building after the manager had met them at the door. These guests were mainly dignitaries from the Basildon Development Corporation, the Basildon Council and major customers. Later, staff and management chatted with them at the buffet laid on in the banking hall. The local directors also mingled amongst the guests. The party began at about four p.m. but as is often the case, the builders were still finishing off many of the fittings right up to the deadline, and they left sawdust and oddments of building materials all around as they were departing. I was given the job of cleaning up, and, having established the route that the chief clerk would take the guests on their conducted tour, I was able to proceed with the vacuum cleaner just ahead of the party. I would disappearing out of one door as the chief clerk led the guests in through another. He would keep talking for as long as he could to give me the chance to finish the next room and move on before he brought them through.

As I left the branch that weekend to return to Hadleigh for a third period within seven years, Stuart Barker, the manager, said to me, "Who knows? It would not surprise me if, one day, you might return to Basildon as manager!" At the time, I thought that his comments were probably made as a jest, tinged with a little sarcasm, but not intended to be unfriendly. I was only a cashier and had no long-term ambition at the time. My main wish was to progress to the post of securities clerk, but his words were to prove to be a prophecy, fifteen years later.

Before leaving this chapter, I have two other events to relate, neither of which really fits into the narrative elsewhere.

The first relates to the inspection teams. As I have described in the early chapters, the inspectors would descend upon a branch without notice well before opening time, and immediately carry out a check of all the cash and of the post-book. The element of surprise was essential, and upon entering a branch, the inspectors hastened to begin their task by pressing the key-holders to accompany them to the strong-room. Others would take over the post-book.

On one occasion the inspector (and I have met the man who led the team) took his team from a country district to check a London branch, as the London teams were over-stretched at the time. The team arrived at the designated branch, knocked on the door, showed their passes and were admitted. The assistant manager and the chief clerk of the branch showed them to the strong-room, and opened the cash safes. As they were checking the bundles of notes, the senior inspector noticed that all the wrappers bore the name XY Bank Limited. It was only while he was asking why this was, that the dreadful reality of the situation revealed itself to him. They were in the *wrong bank!* The door to the branch of Barclays was immediately adjacent to the branch of XY Bank, and they had knocked at the wrong door!

There was confusion and embarrassment on both sides. After all, the XY Bank staff had admitted them and had opened their vaults to them. The poor manager of the XY Bank branch said that he had no option but to report the matter to his head office and, likewise, the Barclays team's senior inspector had to report the incident to the Barclays chief inspector's office.

Another amazing but regular occurrence happened in one of my smaller branches, which I shall not name. We had a customer whose business was usually thriving but often experienced cash flow problems. It was necessary for him to write many cheques for the benefit of his creditors, but there were seldom sufficient funds to meet the cheques when they were presented. A branch accountant would often discuss with a customer which cheques he would like paid against an available balance, and which he would prefer to be returned. This customer, however, was, astoundingly, permitted to come behind the work desk and go through the cheques for himself and then tell the ledger clerk which cheques to pay, and which to return! "Pay that one!" and then, "Return that one, he can wait!" "Better pay that one, it's the landlord," and so on. The irony is that he did this in full view of all the local customers, most of whom knew him quite well but none complained. Needless to say, the branch management was running a grave risk in allowing this to happen. It was fortunate for them that the branch was not the subject of a surprise short inspection (usually about two hours in duration and during business hours) whilst this irregularity was taking place.

Chapter Eight

Into Management: 45 Victoria Avenue, Southend-on-Sea

As I have indicated earlier, my appointment to assistant manager of 45 Victoria Avenue branch in Southend-on-Sea on 2nd July 1965 came as a complete surprise to me and to everyone else, except for the local directors who had made the appointment. My manager, Bert Hattey, was much respected in the district. Before joining the district as manager of 24 High Street, he had come from Minories branch, in the East End where he had been assistant manager. To be the assistant manager of a large East End branch was a much bigger job than that of any assistant manager in the Chelmsford district; indeed, it was a much bigger job than that of many a full branch manger in Chelmsford district. Anyone who worked in the City or in the branches in the East End or West End of London was regarded with a certain awe. They had probably had to deal with bills of exchange, shipping documents, warehousing and many other complicated transactions with the big business houses, such as we in the country only ever read about in text books. Such transactions caused us difficulty when they cropped up merely as questions in the Institute of Bankers' examinations. As well as everybody else, I suspect that Mr Hattey had also expected, and would have welcomed, the appointment of Don Miller as his assistant. I suspect that he had his reservations about my appointment, though he tactfully concealed them and welcomed me in a most friendly manner. Some of the rest of the staff did not hide their reservations, however, and I realised that I would need to prove my right to the job, believing, to be honest, that I had perhaps come too far too soon.

The one person who wanted me to succeed was my father, who was now chief clerk of the Southend Transport office in the new Civic Centre office block in Victoria Avenue, almost immediately opposite the bank. When I was born he was a tram-driver but he had worked his way up through the transport stores department and on to the clerical side.

45 Victoria Avenue was almost brand new when I took up my position. The assistant manager's office was quite large and well appointed with modern, stylish furniture so I really felt that I had arrived. The hand-over from my predecessor was brief, as he was needed to go to his new branch as soon as possible. Management appointments were rather like the sales of residential properties, and each appointment was part of a chain. The appointment at the top of the chain usually followed a retirement or a death, or perhaps the appointment of a senior manager to a head office position. When an appointment was the result of a retirement there was less of a rush to move people up the ladder because all moves could be anticipated well in advance, but a death in office, or an unexpected promotion out of the district, put more urgency into the moves.

My predecessor, Phil Cole, who was to get his own branch, took me to meet some of our most important customers, as well as some of the senior dignitaries of the borough, and of the police, etc. Amongst the top customers was Jack Jones, the owner of Channel Airways, a local air-charter and package-holiday group, operating out of Southend Airport. Not many years before I had taken my Cornish mother-in-law, who was nearly seventy at the time and game for anything, for a sightseeing joy-flight around the local coast line, in an old Auster high-winged monoplane. This was the only aeroplane owned by Jack Jones at that time, and I believe that it was an ex-army machine, from wartime service. It seated four, but mother-in-law was on the large side, and since my wife had opted out there were only the two of us and Jack, the pilot. Jack's wife did all the office work and answered the telephone, but she also had to swing the propeller. From joy-flights, he had progressed to his present company, through flying planes including the old De Havilland Rapide biplanes to and from the Channel Islands, hence the name of the company. From that small beginning about ten years earlier with just one aeroplane, by 1965 he was operating with three or four Vickers Viscount turbo-prop airliners. He was also acquiring hotels in places such as Malta, so that he could offer his customers a complete package holiday from companies under his control. The growth was very commendable to his business acumen.

When Phil took me to be introduced to him, he looked upon me somewhat disdainfully and conducted his conversation with Phil, as if the latter were not leaving. He was anxious to tell Phil how he proposed to purchase one of the then new BA111 jets. These were twin-engined smaller jet airliners, carrying about seventy passengers, but which could halve the flying time to the more common destinations such as Alicante in Spain, thus requiring less aircraft and crew.

At this point, probably unwisely, I felt a need to remind him of my presence, and so made what I had hoped he would have considered to be an erudite comment. I suggested to him that, since he had made his money from buying-up older aircraft from airlines such as Cambrian Airways, from whom he had purchased his Viscounts at a knock-down price, he could proverbially fly them into the ground. He would need a different capital base, however, to start buying brand new expensive jet aircraft. The look that he gave me spoke volumes, and he ignored me for the rest of the meeting, and barely acknowledged me as we took our farewells. The two BA111s, which I believe he purchased on finance, proved a success, but like all ambitious businessmen, a few years later he bit off more than his company could chew when he started to buy, or lease, the larger Tridents. There was a recession in the early seventies, and in common with most travel companies, the company's cash flow was under pressure. Very sadly, the Official Receiver was put in by

Kleinwort-Benson, who had financed the deals, and that was the end of a very successful local enterprise. I was sorry, because I had always admired Jack Jones. My wife and I were watching the BBC *Nine O'Clock News*, when the collapse of the Channel Airways group of companies was announced. As the item was broadcast, the photograph of Jack Jones was shown, full screen. Unfortunately, it was not Jack Jones of Channel Airways, but the other Jack Jones, the General Secretary of the TGWU. This other Jack Jones was at the extreme opposite of the political spectrum to our Jack Jones who was most upset at this final insult added to his injury.

Bert Hattey was due to retire six months after my appointment, and although not winding down in workload, he obviously had his eye upon his retirement date. The forthcoming retirement tended to increase the workload for both of us. He did not want to become too involved in new business that would continue after his retirement, and it was necessary for me to be well versed with our ongoing business, so that I could help the continuity when the new manager arrived. On top of this, for his last few months he had caught a severe dose of influenza, which persisted in plaguing him right through to his final day in the bank.

At that time there had come upon us a sharp recession, and many businesses were having a bad time. Finance companies who had over-stretched themselves with the credit boom of the early 1960s found themselves in trouble and many, even those that were well-known, went into liquidation. The business of one of the branch's major customers, T G Limited, a local finance company, collapsed with terrible financial implications for many people, and not only for local depositors. Basically, it should have been a sound business, and had it kept to financing personal hire purchase for the purchase of cars and furniture and so on, it would probably have survived quite easily. However, the proprietor had decided to pour funds into a new venture to float a free local newspaper. Such newspapers were quite an innovation in those days, and although they are the norm nowadays, they were virtually unheard of in the mid-1960s. The Burroughs family controlled the old-established

Southend Standard and the sister paper, the *Southend Pictorial*, and they proved to be formidable competitors. As with most finance companies, as the proprietor required more and more cash to service the interest and repayments, so he needed to borrow more, and pushed up the interest rate on his deposit accounts to attract additional funds. Inevitably the bubble had burst, and that had happened just after I arrived at 45 Victoria Avenue.

There was about one week's notice of the collapse. The bank stood to lose a substantial sum on a loan to another company within the group, and we had no security. In order to obtain more money and more time from the bank, the proprietor had deposited some deeds with the branch as a show of faith, but he had refused to have the company seal a charge to the bank over the deeds. Fortunately, he did indicate in the letter accompanying the deeds that he was depositing them as security in consideration of the additional facility. Without a formal completed charge registered at Company's House, however, the security would have been forfeit to any eventual receiver or liquidator. I was fairly fresh from my securities' course of 1963, and from my studying for Part II of the Institute exams. Thus I realised that it was possible to register an Oral Charge provided that there was some written evidence available to indicate that the land was intended to be security for a loan. The company's letter served the bank's needs in this respect. I therefore had the branch security team rushing around arranging to get this charge in time to protect our loan. The main difficulty was that the Head Office Stamping Department, who dealt with these matters, were totally unfamiliar with the process, and Inspection Department had to assist, but they came up trumps and we had our security registered in time.

When the company collapsed it was a terrible business. Some savers, widows and the like, had lost all their life savings. I received a phone call from Hong Kong, which was a very exceptional occurrence in those days. The poor man at the other end of the line had been living upon the income of his investment of ninety thousand pounds in the company, his entire fortune! It was heartbreaking to hear all the tales of disaster, and I almost had a bad conscience for saving the bank's twenty thousand pounds, but had I not done so, there still would have been nothing left to pay the investors, or any other creditor. To get our funds back we had to sell the deeds of the property and the proceeds only just covered our exposure and the legal fees. When the proprietor discovered that the bank had managed to protect itself with its security after all, he telephoned me and berated me for what I had done.

My salary was approximately one thousand five hundred and seventy-five pounds per annum. Bert Hattey's was probably in the region of four thousand pounds per annum, which was a handsome sum at the time. Upon retirement at age sixty, after forty years or more in the bank, he would have qualified for a pension of forty-sixtieths of his final pay, which would have given him two thirds of four thousand pounds, or just under two thousand seven hundred pounds per annum. Most likely, he would have commuted a fairly large sum which he could have used to pay off any home-loan which he may have had outstanding or, alternatively, to have had a sum to invest in order to supplement his income. The result would have meant that his eventual pension would probably have been in the region of two thousand pounds per annum. It seemed to be a lot of money then, but since Bert was fortunate enough to draw his pension until he recently died at the age of about ninety-two, it would have seemed a pittance in the latter years. Pensions in those days were not indexed-linked. Although some increases have been given to staff who retired before the end of the 1960s, this, at one time, handsome pension would have deteriorated drastically at the end because of the rapid inflation experienced in the years between. There were, and still are, many of the older retired staff who have fallen on hard times due only to having been unlucky in the date upon which they were born.

What annoyed me at the time was the fact that our chief clerk, who did not exert himself unduly, received a higher salary than me because of his age. He was about ten years older than me. In addition, he was entitled to receive overtime payments whereas manager grades were not.

Whilst at 45 Victoria Avenue, I worked a great deal of overtime. Before Bert Hattey left I often worked late on managerial duties, but later, in the time of the new manager, a new system in posting ledgers and statements was introduced called "Single-Shot Posting". I shall not bore the reader with details, but, suffice to say it was a system introduced by the Organisation and Methods Department, which was totally impracticable. When we complained they sent one of their troubleshooters down to prove that it was the branch that was at fault and not the system. We had some very bright younger members in our machine-room and we enlisted them to form a team to meet the troubleshooter. Between us we destroyed this poor man's case so that he had to give up all attempts to convince us of the efficiency of the system. He then confessed that Head Office wanted the system, which was really a step on the road to computerisation of the bank's book-keeping system, and we had no alternative but to persevere. This resulted in much late working which took its toll on the morale of the machine-room staff. The new manager and I decided to lead the way, and we went into the machine-room at the end of each day to assist with any menial tasks, such as filing away cheques or ledger sheets or whatever. Often it was eight p.m. before we could leave, especially on Friday evenings or at the end of the month.

Our new manager was Ken Williams, a brilliant man, who at one time had been chief clerk at 24 High Street just after I had returned from the navy. I shall refer to him often as I relate my tale, but among our machine-room supervisors we had a rather severe but highly efficient lady by the name of Sheila Hall. Each day, around five o'clock, Ken would ask me if the work was finished and correct. "I don't know," I would reply, "you had better ask Sheila!"

"*You* ask her!" he would command, and we would have a good laugh since neither of us wanted to ask Sheila, because of the fiery response we would receive if things were not going well.

My previous feelings about being a misfit in the bank had come to the fore again when I had joined 45 Victoria Avenue branch, and had sensed that senior staff, including the chief clerk, had doubted me to be up to the job. However, the taking of the oral charge, something that few of the security staff knew to be possible, did raise me a little in their esteem. The news, however, that, upon the retirement of Bert Hattey, Ken Williams was to come up from 108 High Street where he was manager, stifled any confidence that I might have regained. My promotion had been fairly rapid, and at times I recognised the lack of experience in lower jobs that lay behind me, and would feel myself to be at a disadvantage.

"Well, Denis Sherringham," I said to myself, "if anybody is sure to rumble you, it will be Ken Williams!"

Ken was a friendly man with a razor-sharp banking brain, but I knew that he would not tolerate an incompetent assistant manager. His moving into 45 Victoria Avenue had been entirely logical, because it was the second part of the operation to transfer all the business accounts from the two old main branches in the High Street to 45 Victoria Avenue. Obviously the branch had needed time in which to absorb the business brought in upon the transfer of Bert Hattey from 24 High Street. In those days, it was frowned upon for managers to encourage account holders to follow them from their old branch to the new one. It could mean that his replacement to the branch found that he had a much smaller branch to manage than he had been promised, especially if really large accounts had followed the previous manager. In the case of Bert Hattey and Ken Williams the opposite strategy applied.

I need not have worried since Ken and I got along very well. It may have been better for me if I could have remained with him and learned from his excellent example.

With regard to taking rather unusual charges, I had another occasion to cause eyebrows to be raised. This was the result of my being called upon by a customer of the name of John Prime. John was a Thames barge enthusiast, and, together with some friends who were all competent, they wanted to buy a Thames barge by the name of *Kitty*. They proposed to fit her out for the purpose of taking schoolchildren on estuary and coastal voyages lasting up to a week. His colleagues in the venture were John Fairbrother, typically bearded but quite a young man, and one of the few remaining fully certificated barge skippers operating trading barges, and the other was a fully qualified working shipwright. John Prime and his wife, June, already owned another barge, the *Gipping,* which was lying in a berth alongside the quay at Maldon, Essex. This barge was their home, and had been fitted with central heating and a bathroom with hot and cold water and all mod cons. It was a really cosy home with several rooms and with stacks of space. These barges had been built around ninety years previously, i.e. about 1860-1870, and each one was constructed around an enormous pine log keel of about ninety feet in length and about three to four feet diameter.

John and his pals wanted to form a company to buy the *Kitty* and to partition the enormous hold in order to provide sleeping and dining accommodation for around fifteen children plus the accompanying schoolteachers. The Board of Trade would license the vessels but only once an auxiliary engine had been fitted for safety reasons. The installing of an engine and a propeller to a Thames barge was sheer sacrilege to the enthusiast, but, in order to preserve the barges and to keep them sailing, "beggars could not be choosers", and so they had acquiesced. The schools who were to be their clients were mainly from the East End, from the Borough of Newham in particular, and from other boroughs in that area.

There was already one barge in operation offering these school trips. This was the *Memory*, run by other fully qualified barge operators. The children loved the experience and they would sail from Maldon around to the Thames Estuary, perhaps to Southend Pier, or to Sheerness. The distances that they could sail in the time or whether or not they were able to leave the River Blackwater depended upon weather conditions. They slept in cosy bunks and the heating came from the old-fashioned coal or coke stove, upon which they also fried their own breakfasts of egg and bacon and the like. The voyage was like sea-going camping, and during the day they would help to sail the barge. They would steer it, winch the leeboards up and down, and give a hand to hoist and set the sails.

As it was always my policy to see things at first hand wherever possible, I attended a board meeting held in John and June's home, the *Gipping,* where I got to know all the directors much better. A fish and chip supper accompanied by giant mugs of tea was served as we chatted things over. I decided to help them, but I needed to take a marine mortgage over *Gipping,* not over *Kitty,* and John and June agreed.

I returned to the branch next day and told the securities clerks to draw-up a marine mortgage, which, not surprisingly, they had never done before. I sent off a valuation form to the manager of our Maldon branch. Upon receipt of this request, he telephoned me, and asked me a few questions about the barge, and it was obvious that he had never been asked to value one before. However, he sent huge doubts racing around my mind when he said, "Well, I suppose it is all right, but I suspect that if I were to prod it with my penknife, the knife would go right through the hull!" I began to have serious misgivings about my judgement.

The next telephone call came from the head of Barclays Shipping Department, and this call added to my worries. When asking me about the venture, he said very casually, "Very interesting! I have been through our records and this is the *oldest* vessel, by far, over which we have ever taken a marine mortgage!" My heart sank. As it turned out, I had nothing to worry about. The venture was a great success, and the lending was repaid before the agreed expiry date.

John and June, and my wife and I are still good friends and still meet up occasionally. They have long since sold both barges. Only recently, in the summer of 1998, I saw the *Kitty,* now with her hull painted green, sailing in a match against a flotilla of other barges at the Cowes Regatta. She was the subject of my first published article, "Who Led Kitty Up The River?", which I wrote at the time for the Barclays in-house staff magazine, the *Spread Eagle.* This was written after I had been taken aboard for the Thames Barge Match from Southend Pier. Unfortunately somebody in the committee boat had made an error and sent us round the wrong buoy, putting us virtually out of the race. I was rather flattered when the Port of London Authority sought permission to reprint the article in their magazine. Of course permission was granted! Sadly, I think that the *Gipping*, after being sold on by John and June, passed through several other pairs of hands until it fell into disrepair and disintegrated. A similar fate befell the *Memory*, so I am informed.

On another occasion, I nearly made a gaff, when, having been given the wrong information prior to an interview, I almost adopted a completely wrong attitude toward the person sitting in front of me. There had been much local publicity about a man by the name of Williams, who wanted to become involved in a ferry service to run from Southend Pier to Kent. Other than what had been written in the local and national press about his business operations, I had no first-hand knowledge of whether or not he was the rogue that the press made him out to be. However, when the securities clerks told me that he wanted to see me, I immediately cautioned myself to be on my guard. He was not one of our customers, and I could only surmise that he would be the type to come in to open an account, and, at the same time, try to bemuse me with tales about the wonderful prospects of his proposed enterprise.

The person who was shown in to my room, however, was far from what I had expected. He was a mild-mannered, cultured type, and as soon as he had begun to speak he must have noticed the quizzical look in my eye. "Is there something wrong?" he asked.

"Aren't you Mr Williams of X Marine?" I stammered querulously.

"No, I am Chief Constable Williamson of Durham police."

I was dumbfounded. It turned out that he had come to investigate the affairs of our local chief constable, who had been suspended from his duties for misusing police facilities for his own benefit. Our chief constable was a much-liked man, locally, and the general opinion was that he was being punished for overstepping the mark with his superiors on the council, but that was only local gossip at the time.

Chief Constable Williamson wanted access to certain bank accounts and, as was to be expected from a man in his position, he had obtained all the necessary legal authorities to permit himself and his officers this access.

When he left, I was still bemused. The securities clerks still maintained that the appointment had been made for the Mr Williams of X Marine, at the same time that Chief Constable Williamson had arrived, and they suspected that Mr Williams had just not turned up, and that the whole thing had been a coincidence. To this day, I still wonder if that had been the case, but have I never regretted not having to meet the ebullient Mr Williams of X Marine!

Through 1965 to early 1966, I had only a very limited knowledge of the incoming vogue of Management Accountancy, and of Management by Objectives. These skills both involved forecasting, budgeting, cash flow forecasts, and break-even points and the rest. One day I was visited by a number of professional gentlemen from a company that occupied offices situated above the branch in the same high-rise office block. The company, about which I knew very little, had a strange name which ended in "Engineering Limited", and, not having dealt with them before, I suspected that they were, as implied, engineers of some sort. I had not reflected upon the various meanings that the word "engineer" could convey.

There were about six of them, and when they had been shown to seats in front of my desk, and after my secretary had served tea and biscuits, I asked, "Well, gentlemen, can you tell me something about your business?" They completely surprised me by pointing out that they were all financial accountants of one sort or another. "Well," I ventured, "who does the engineering?"

It was their turn to look perplexed, and then with a smile, the leader explained, "There is no physical engineering, as such. We are financial consultants, and we help companies to engineer their businesses to achieve the maximum potential."

He then went on to explain the ramifications of management accounting, and how it could be used to plan ahead and to predict profitability and to avoid financial pitfalls. When he had finished, I was flabbergasted. "Do you mean to tell me that you go about advising businesses how to remain solvent, when it is now apparent that you have asked for this meeting to persuade me to pay your salaries for this month? All the evidence is that *your company* is insolvent!" I stated rather forcibly. "No, gentlemen, I cannot help you. You must go to the chairman of your parent company for your money." One thing that I did know was that the company was Dutch-owned, and I was not prepared to rely upon the guarantees or promises of persons whom I did not know, and who were also resident overseas. Their Dutch board of directors did not help them, and shortly afterwards the company folded.

This experience taught me to regard management accounting with a certain degree of suspicion. It is a good tool, if used properly by capable people, but it is not a panacea for all financial ills. I was, and still am a believer in the old banking adage, "Know your customer" – *only then* one can look at his (or her) financial projections.

As I mentioned earlier, Bert Hattey had come into the Chelmsford district from Minories branch in the London Eastern district. Whilst he was working in London he established business links with members of the ultra-orthodox Jewish community, who mainly lived in the Stamford Hill and Stoke Newington areas of London. Many of these very well educated gentlemen had various business interests, but most had a sideline in property. Some concentrated entirely in property, and built up huge property empires, and I shall deal with this in more detail in the next chapter. In accordance with their religious customs, these gentlemen wore long black overcoats and black homburg hats. All were bearded and had peots, which were long side-whiskers, in accordance with the Judaic law, and as a result they were generally known as "the beards" by less orthodox Jewish people and by gentiles, alike. They were mostly courteous and generous, giving huge sums from their income to charity. Each community funded the religious schools and synagogues in its area.

If they established a good business relationship with their bank manager, be he with Barclays or any other bank, they would follow that manager to all the future branches that he might manage. Usually they would not transfer their bank accounts, which were mostly in the names of small limited companies, but would open new ones at the branch manager's new branch, and in this way their network would spread like a spider's web across the country.

When Bert Hattey had come from Minories branch where he was assistant manager, he brought just one such customer with him, a Mr G, whose main business was in trading commercial diamonds. As with most of the *frum*, (the Yiddish word for the ultra-orthodox sect), he spoke with an accent, slightly German in intonation, and it was not always easy to comprehend what he said. That the securities clerks were rather in awe of him, there was no doubt. I could sense that they were going to enjoy my first confrontation with Mr G, and I think that they probably had good reason. I too found him difficult to understand, both in his manner of speaking, and also with regard to his business dealings and methods. He was a kindly and friendly man, but I would shudder when I saw his name on my appointments list.

During this time, I was sent on my Stage III Course at the Bank Management College, which was then resident at The Selsdon Court Hotel in Sanderstead, Surrey, where there was a well-known golf course of tournament standard. This course was for newly appointed managers and assistant managers. At the end of the course, we were entertained to a buffet reception by the general manager, staff at 54 Lombard Street. At that time the general manager, staff was none other than Mr Cecil Ling, who had been my manager at 24 High Street shortly after my return from the navy. He circulated amongst small groups and individuals from those on the course, and eventually came my turn.

"I think that we must break the mould of management staff staying in one district for the full duration of their careers," he stated. "They should be willing to transfer from district to district in order to gain promotion."

Being somewhat in awe of being spoken to by a general manager, despite the fact that he was the same man who had once complimented me on the way I had run the fifth till at 24 High Street in the busy summer months, I heartily agreed. I had not given much thought to the problems for a family with children at school having to up its roots and travel, perhaps the length of the country, to a new home in strange surroundings. I had taken the coward's way out, and it was to rebound upon me not long afterwards. This interview had taken place in April 1966, and in October 1966 I was transferred to be assistant manager of Stepney branch. Ironically, the last customer I had interviewed before leaving was none other than Mr G. He bid me a fond farewell and wished me all the best for my future. I felt such a sense of relief in having escaped from his clutches!

By this time, of course, Bert Hattey had retired, and Ken Williams was my manager. He was a friendly outgoing sort, and, when we discussed my move, he said that I was going to notice a vast difference in banking between the East End and the country. My move was scheduled for about three weeks after I had been advised of it, and I had to go to Head Office to see the general managers to receive my appointment, officially. This was a formality then, but stories were told of appointees failing their interviews and losing their promotions as a result of an unfortunate chance remark, or because one of the general managers had been in a bad mood on the day. When I arrived at Head Office, I met up with another interviewee, a manager, who was getting promotion to a large branch on the Isle of Wight.

"Where are you off to?" he asked.

"I am switching from assistant manager in Southend to assistant manager in Stepney."

"What! With Joe Holmes?" he queried. "You had better take your drinking boots!" and with that worrying remark he was summoned for his first interview. My interviews were satisfactory, despite the irritation of the general manager who asked me whether or not customers should be billed for their bank charges, as I have mentioned earlier.

Still a bit concerned by the attitude of the manager who was destined for better things in the Isle of Wight, I returned to 45 Victoria Avenue, and had another chat with Ken Williams.

"Well, now that your appointment is confirmed, why don't you telephone your new boss, and arrange to go to see him at Stepney branch?" It was a sound suggestion, and Ken was prepared to give me the time off to go, so I decided that was what I would do. I tried on numerous occasions to get through to Mr Holmes on the telephone, but I could never get beyond the blind telephonist who manned the switchboard. Either Mr Holmes was not in or he was too busy to talk to me. One morning, with still just over a week to go, I managed to speak to the great man.

"Mr Holmes?" I asked, somewhat nervously. "Yes?" came the abrupt reply. It is surprising how much can be conveyed in one short word, but I could sense that he did not really wish to be bothered with me.

"I am to be your new assistant manager... " I began.

"Well, what about it?" came his pointed reply.

"Well, I wondered if I might come up to introduce myself and also to meet you and to see the branch."

"What is the point of that? We shall see all that we want to see of each other, when you get here!" and with that he put the phone down. I was to learn that, Joe, as I have always known him since, had periods of manic depression, and yet he was one of the most enigmatic characters that I was ever to meet in my life.

I told Ken about the call; he could only shrug his shoulders by way of a resigned gesture, and it was with great foreboding that I took my leave of 45 Victoria Avenue branch.

Chapter Nine

Introduction to Stepney Branch

I was still carrying this foreboding as I alighted from the slam-door single compartment of the Southend to Fenchurch Street train, at Stepney station. Today, it is called, more appropriately, Limehouse, where it links with the recently built Docklands Light Railway, the DLR, which connects the City to Canary Wharf, the City Airport, and Greenwich, by way of the foot-tunnel from Island Gardens Station. All these developments were, during my time at Stepney branch, some twenty years away.

I walked up the Commercial Road, at about eight-thirty a.m., dodging the spittle and the dog mess that covered much of the paving stones, towards one of the highest profit earning branches outside the major City and West End offices. It was most depressing especially as, on this cold morning of late October, it was also drizzling. For the two and a half years that I made this morning journey toward the branch, I never enjoyed it any better. When I arrived at the portals of 451 Commercial Road, I found an almost dilapidated building, dating from the previous century. It stood on Commercial Road, on the corner with Jamaica Street, and, until just prior to my arrival, had let out its upstairs offices to a firm of solicitors. By the time that I started to work there, the building had been condemned. The upper rooms were vacant or used by the branch for storage, except for one room which was used by the standing-orders clerk, and another as a staff room, with a small kitchen in a third. The whole place was run-down and old-fashioned, and smelt musty, especially when climbing the old wooden staircase.

On arrival, I was shown to the assistant manager's room, to await the arrival of my predecessor, when we would commence our two-day hand-over. As I approached the assistant manager's room, which was an annex to the manager's room, I noticed the inscription in old-fashioned ornate gold leaf lettering on the glass window of the door, "Waiting Room".

When Jim Groves, my predecessor arrived, he proved to be a rather chubby and cheerful Londoner. He met me in a friendly way, but I felt right out of my depth and my spirits were not raised when I was introduced to the other senior staff. The chief clerk was about my age and, except for his National Service, had spent his working life in London Eastern district branches. He came, I discovered, from Thorpe Bay, which is to the east of the town centre of Southend-on-Sea and where I now live. At that time I was living in Leigh-on-Sea, at the western end of the borough. The chief clerk showed no wish to be friendly, and I felt from the start that he was going to show me who was the more dominant of the two of us. Although we came to get on all right eventually, we were never close friends and seldom travelled up or down in the train together. This was partly because of the fact that our hours were not compatible. It was obvious that he and the rest of the staff considered that my appointment from "the sticks", as they liked to call country districts, was a mistake. It was rather like my arrival at 45 Victoria Avenue, all over again. The senior securities clerk, Don Cottle, was in his late fifties, and had been demoted from a chief clerk's job at one of the larger Ilford branches. He was one of those types who was brilliant as a securities clerk, but who was in the wrong job when asked to become an office manager and a controller of staff. As a securities clerk, he was second to none, and the fact that Joe regarded him so, was the highest of accolades. He was a tall, slim, grey-haired, cynical type with a droll, rather sarcastic sense of humour, especially toward those whom he regarded as young upstarts. Yet he was not unfriendly and I came to like him and to respect him very much. The rest of the staff mostly had that easy-going casual air of the East Enders, which nearly all of them were. I could still sense that they did not really think that I would last. That "misfit" feeling, that dogged me throughout my career, had come to the fore again.

When Joe arrived, I was introduced to him at the "opening of-the-post ceremony", which was to be part of my daily ritual from then on. Each morning we would be brought cups of coffee by the messenger, Arthur. Actually, I never heard him called Arthur by anyone, not even by himself! He was known to everyone as "Arfer", and he was Joe's treasure. Occasionally, but not often, he had to don his navy blue coat and bowler hat and go out on a message to Local Head Office at London Wall Buildings, or to the City. Usually he wore a shabby, none-too-clean, brown dust coat, similar to that worn by proprietors of ironmongers' shops. He was the typical London cockney, always cheerful, and although he would moan a bit now and then, he never really had a bad word for anyone. The only disturbing thing about Arfer was his scullery in the basement of the branch. Arfer used to clean the branch during the day, and he could be seen going around the various areas with his mop and bucket, or polishing up the numerous brass door handles and bits and pieces. His bucket did not bear close inspection. It contained dirty water with scum floating on the top. It seemed that his "cleaning" actually applied more dirt and grease than it removed. After he had finished he would dispose of the water into the old butler sink in his scullery. This sink was yellow with age and heavily chipped. After throwing away the dirty cleaning water, he would then wash up the cups and saucers. Most of the staff drank from old chipped mugs, which should have been thrown out long before. Joe's drinks glasses were washed in the same sink and in the same fashion. Hygiene was not a word in Arfer's vocabulary but Joe and the rest of the staff just seemed to accept it as the norm, and I was not in a position to do anything about it until much later.

I cannot remember what I had imagined Joe to look like before we met, and I suspect that I had no real idea what to expect, but when he came into the branch that morning, I was surprisingly impressed. This man who had the reputation of being a Hercules amongst drinkers, was silver-haired, tall and elegant, and he wore the regulation bowler hat, and carried, together with his rolled silk umbrella and kid gloves, a copy of *The Times* newspaper. This was the old *Times* before the Murdoch group bought it out, after its many industrial disputes through its closed-shop policy union. Joe was the epitome of a City gentleman, and I was to have many an argument with him because I refused to wear a bowler hat, and it was one issue on which I was not prepared to yield, and I never did.

Our first meeting was, to my relief, most affable. On his good days, he was a very kindly and courteous man and fond of a joke, but on his bad days...! I shall say no more about Joe at this time, as I shall devote a chapter to the stories about him, which are legion. At this stage, I wish to concentrate upon those early days at Stepney.

As was the usual practice, Jim Groves, my predecessor, arranged either for certain important customers to call to meet me and to say farewell to him, or he whisked me off to see others. He also spent a great deal of time on the telephone arranging his farewell party, mainly for staff but also to include a few customers, at the Three Swedish Crowns pub at Wapping, to be held the next evening. At that time *Till Death Do Us Part* was the latest comedy hit-show and close to the Three Swedish Crowns was Garnet Street, in which stood a row of terraced houses which had been restored to a high standard by the BBC. In this row was the house in which the Garnets were purported to live. It was from the name of this street that the late Johnny Speight had adopted the name of Alf Garnet for his anti-hero in his masterpiece.

Amongst the customers introduced to me were several of the *frum* community, and one of those given much prominence was Rabbi Pinter, the principle of the Yesodeh Atorah School, one of the leading orthodox Jewish schools in London. Rabbi Pinter was, like so many others of his community, into property deals. He and Jim Groves got on very well together, but business relations between the rabbi and myself were to be less warm, which was unusual because

I got on very well with most of the many other *frum* customers on our books.

It was such a hectic day, and we had a lunch consisting of a hot pie and a pint of ale at the Exmouth Arms, which was a delightful old pub in Exmouth Street, about two roads up the Commercial Road from Jamaica Street. It was over one hundred years old, and was no modern gin palace, but was full of antique mirrors advertising ancient ales in ornamental lettering and old-fashioned polished benches. Later, when the whole area was to be demolished for redevelopment, John Betjeman, the poet laureate, had led a group which had saved this beautiful old pub, and had it isolated upon an "island" – like an oasis amongst all the garish modern buildings. In the late 1960s, before all the redevelopment, the dockers from the local London docks, which sadly are no more, heavily frequented it. During my time at Stepney, a hot pie and half-a-pint of ale at the Exmouth Arms, was to be my usual lunch-time fare, although a sandwich or a beigel and a cup of Arfer's tea at my desk was not uncommon on busy days.

Around six p.m. that day I managed to catch a train home and I arrived indoors at about eight p.m.

"How did you get on on your first day, dear?" asked my wife, Joyce.

"Just don't ask me!" I replied somewhat discourteously.

Jim had considered his handing-over duties to have been completed by the end of my first day, and he devoted the second day entirely to taking his leave of many of his favourites from amongst the branch customers and to completing arrangements and invitations to his party. None of the orthodox customers would come for religious reasons, but nearly the whole customer base was Jewish and many were not extremely religious. Some would go to *Shul*, as the Synagogue was known, on a Saturday, but many others did not.

I therefore found myself thrown in at the deep-end on the second morning. My first job was to take over the reserve of bank notes in the safe in the strong-room. This meant that as one of two key-holders, I had to count the reserve, and agree it with the figures shown in the Reserve Book and sign for it, together with the other key-holder, who would be the first cashier or perhaps the chief clerk. Checking the reserve was not as onerous as it might sound, because, as I have already explained, all the notes to be put to reserve had to be packaged and sealed and signed by the cashier from whose till they had come, and by the checker. Provided each packet was double-signed and sealed, the reserve key-holders were able to accept them at their face value. Compared to Southend-on-Sea, Stepney had far less demand for cash and little changed hands, other than for wages, and so the reserve was much smaller than I had been used to. What did take my breath away was the amount of liquor in the strong-room. There were crates of whisky, brandy and gin mainly but there were also one or two cases of champagne and other wines. This drink came from all the bottles given to Joe at Christmas time, mainly from the orthodox customers. When I arrived it was late October and yet there were still many crates. By then the champagne which remained had been reduced down to what the labels declared to be "Israel's Finest and Most Expensive", because all the Bollinger and the Moet and Chandon had long since been consumed. I was to discover that this Israeli "champagne" did not live up to the claim on the label by any stretch of the imagination! I told my wife that, had I been a burglar who had successfully broken into the strong-room, I would have left the cash and taken the booze! I shall have more to say about where the booze came from in a later chapter.

Reverting to the morning of my second day at the branch, once I had returned to my desk, I found four extract books awaiting me. An extract book was rather like a hard-covered exercise book ruled up in columns resembling a cashbook. There was one for each of our four main property-owning customers. Each of these customers had a separate property company for each property that it owned. In the smallest group of the four customers were about fifty limited companies, and in the largest there were about one hundred and forty. The other two groups each had something in between these two extremes. These customers were all *frum*. Mr B was the largest; Mr F W was next, Mr E was third and Mr F, the son-in-law of Mr E was fourth. Their individual personal commitments were high when all the balances within their groups were added up, because each had given his personal guarantee for all borrowings as well as having charged the title deeds of all the properties as security for the loans made against them. I discovered the reason why all these groups had arisen. In the bank a branch manager had a personal discretion for lending either on a secured or on an unsecured basis. Let us say that if the discretion had been for five thousand pound for secured lending, then it would probably have been about two thousand pounds for unsecured lending. That is what a manager could lend an individual customer without referring to his local head office, but, if that individual owned a limited company, then that limited company, which in law was regarded as a separate entity, could also borrow in its own right. Therefore if the lending to the company had been against the deeds of a property, and, provided that the sole director had not personally guaranteed the debt, the branch manager could, in effect, have lent twice his secured discretion to the same person. He would not have been required to obtain sanction from his local head office. Many people, not least the Jewish orthodox community, made it a point to discover the lending discretion of their branch manager. By using the ploy of creating a limited company for each property purchased, they could soon be borrowing very large sums of money. Each loan would be serviced from the rents received from the tenants of the property secured to the bank. All went smoothly until the total amounts being lent to individuals by this method had become rather alarming, and somebody at a higher level had decided to put a stop to this practice. It had been decreed that such groupings were not to be considered to be allowable at a branch manager's discretion. From then on each group had to be subject to local head office sanction, or, in the case of some extremely large groups, subject to head office control. It was therefore the job of the assistant manager at Stepney, and at other branches with similar groups to look through all the balances to see that all individual companies accounts were within their lending arrangements as well as the group being within the overall arrangement. I was beginning to learn what East End banking was all about! Bills of exchange and shipping documents were to play only a very small role in my daily tasks.

However, having struggled through the four extract books of balances and totalled positions for the major groups in the branch, I was presented with another extract book from the standing orders clerk. Whenever a loan was granted, an authority would be taken to debit the current account of the customer with the amount of the periodic repayment, usually on a given day each month, and to credit the amount to reduce the loan account. For internal transfers, a red debit card was raised to debit the current account, and a green credit card was raised to credit the loan balance. This was satisfactory provided that there were funds available on the current account to meet the debit when it fell due. If there were insufficient funds a decision had to be made on whether to put the voucher through, thus creating or increasing an overdraft on the current account, or to hold the repayment back until funds became available. It would probably be necessary to write to the customer, or in some cases to telephone. On this first morning I was confronted with a book full of these unpaid repayments. Many of them had been outstanding unpaid for months. Where was I to start? The first thing was to look on the information sheets. I learned that these were kept under the counter, and so I made my way into the banking hall. The information sheets were loose cards in alphabetical groups, with each group being in a separate box. I bent down and reached for A-Ch, or whatever the first box contained but as I stood up a familiar voice greeted me from the other side of the counter.

"Good morning, Mr Sherringham!" My heart sank! It could not be, but it was...Mr G! The very Mr G I had been so pleased to bid farewell to on the previous Friday. Not once on that, or on any occasion, had he let it be known to me that he also banked at Stepney! I would be seeing a lot more of Mr G!

The East End branches, and I suspect, most London branches had been placed on the first fully operational computer system used in the bank. It was known as the

EMI-dec system, or, as it was later to become known, "the old steam computer". This system provided the branches with two printouts a day. The first showed the position after the automatic posting of the clearing, and arrived at the branch around eleven a.m. The second was a full printout after all the day's work had also been printed, but did not arrive until the next morning. Most branches were prepared to examine the clearing list to check if there were any large amounts that might give cause for concern in any way, and which might warrant early enquiry. Otherwise they were content to await the second list before returning cheques for lack of funds as "late returns" on the day following presentation. By the rules of the Clearing House, all late returns were supposed to be telephoned through to the bank and branch that had collected the cheque. Because so many cheques became subject to late return, many branches turned a blind eye to this ruling, and eventually the rules were changed to accept the modern needs and practices. Joe would have none of this in his branch, so Don Cottle was detailed to rework all the balances at the end of the day's work so that cheques could be returned on the same evening if necessary. This, of course, caused a great deal of extra work, and, if the person reworking the balance was careless or was not given all the day's work applying to every account, mistakes could arise. It was for this reason the job was designated to Don Cottle, whose immaculate attention to detail almost eliminated such errors. Of course, this daily process defeated the whole object of computerising the book-keeping.

So, as well as the group balances books, the standing order refer books, I was confronted with the daily clearing refer list plus, later in the day, the full refer list. These lists could be run through rather quickly when the referee had been doing the job for a few months and was familiar with all the accounts that caused problems. Even then, however, a new name appearing in the refer book would cause extra work in assessing whether or not a cheque should be paid or returned. Full checks had to be made to see if the bank could have been at fault in any way. Had a limit for an overdraft been agreed, but not marked against the account?

Had the account holder other accounts, either current or deposit? Were we holding valuable securities that would have been an indication of wealth? Should the customer be telephoned? Should we take the risk to pay the cheque, or should we return it "Refer to Drawer" or "Refer to Drawer – Please Represent"? All these questions needed to be asked, and information sheets and other accounts and securities sheets checked before action was taken.

Well, for me, on that first day, it was sheer turmoil. The rest of the staff who should have helped to advise me, including the chief clerk, even Don Cottle, seemed to be indifferent to my dilemma. I was the assistant manager and it was my job, so I had better get on with it, and they were too busy, anyway! Or so the attitude appeared to be. How I struggled through that day, I just cannot remember. My head seemed to be in a whirl, especially as I was frequently called to meet a customer as well. How I wished that I had never entered banking as a career!

Eventually the day came to an end and by six p.m. staff were being assembled for Jim Grove's farewell presentation and a short speech by Joe Holmes. Many of Jim's bank friends had come to the branch for the occasion, before heading in a group to the Three Swedish Crowns pub in Wapping for the party. In the group, whom I met for the first time, were assistant managers from the other large and mostly local branches. At first I suspected that I should not be welcomed as I was a usurper having arrived from a country branch to take away a plum job in the East End, but it was not like that. I even felt that there was too much warmth in their welcome! I really suspected that they were all very grateful for not having been switched to Stepney from their more comfortable first appointments.

We all made our way to Wapping, and there I met Freddie Croasdell, manager of the smaller branch farther up the Commercial Road at number 140. Freddie, like myself, was living in Leigh-on-Sea, but he lived in the more exclusive area close to Belfairs Golf Course, where he still resides to this day. In 1998 my wife and I had the pleasure of attending his ninetieth birthday. In 1966 he was a short, well built man, in his late fifties. He always wore his bowler hat when out and about in London, and with his rosy cheeks, and in his dark blue overcoat, he very much resembled Mr Pickwick. He had become manager of 140 Commercial Road about five years earlier, having taken over from Joe Holmes, who had been promoted to manage the main Stepney branch. Contrary to Stepney, the business at 140 Commercial Road was mainly Muslim, as opposed to Jewish. He had many Arab or Pakistani customers. Sadly both Stepney and 140 Commercial Road branches have been closed, and the old Stepney branch has been demolished. A brand new Stepney branch was built in the later 1970s, but that too was closed in the early 1990s, as part of the bank's new grouping policy. When I had first arrived at the old Stepney branch, I had turned-up the original lease, which had been drawn up for the freeholder around the turn of the century. The lease was for ninety-nine years at a continuing rent for the whole period of seventy-five pounds per annum! Having sub-leased the upper floors to solicitors, and to other professional people, the bank must have run at a considerable profit for many years on the rent alone.

After the party, which was more about drinking than anything else, Freddie and I managed to slip away. Freddie's wife, who sadly died a few years ago, was not happy when Freddie was waylaid to go drinking, especially with Joe, but more of that later.

On our way home in the train, Freddie asked me what I thought of my appointment. "I shan't last three weeks!" I predicted with some feeling.

Chapter Ten

Settling In at Stepney

It took me weeks to settle into this new environment, and into what amounted to a new way of life. I had to meet so many new customers, of whom very many were unique to the areas where the Jewish orthodox communities thrived. Besides London, these communities were also strong in other cities such as Leeds and Manchester, and many of our customers seemed to have a foot in these other communities as well.

At the time of my arrival, one of the Sunday newspapers was having a field day exposing a certain property dealer, a Mr Rackman, whose name has since been synonymous with the worst kind of landlord. Some of his relations banked with us, but they were not like their more notorious relative, or so they assured us. Some of our bigger property owners controlled very large blocks of flats, and among them were the Freshwater Group, of which we had a portion of the business, but whose main accounts were maintained at large branches such as Cambridge Circus. I was usually in daily contact with the manager or assistant manager of that and the other branches, when we would discuss the overall situation between the group and the bank. When I needed to telephone the head office of the Freshwater Group, I would usually talk to the American son-in-law of Mr Freshwater, a Mr Stern. Mr Stern was later to become known as "Britain's largest bankrupt", when he was sued for about two and a half million pounds by the National Westminster Bank, in the 1970s. Two and a half million pounds would not be considered to be such an astronomical sum in these days as it was then.

Our largest property developer was a Mr B, who together with his father sent very large donations to Jewish charities based in New York. He had numerous properties and was generally regarded to be the headman and benefactor of his community. In addition to banking with us, Mr B had many banking accounts and facilities all over London, and probably elsewhere, not only with Barclays but with all the main clearing banks. He probably had accounts and facilities with the smaller banks as well. In addition to facilities for himself and for his many companies, he guaranteed loans and overdrafts for the accounts of many in his community, mainly for their various businesses rather than for their acquisition of property, although that was not unknown. So often one of the orthodox community would make an appointment to see Joe or myself. He may or may not have had an account, but he would usually want a facility of about five hundred pounds, sometimes more.

"How can you secure this facility?" we would ask, because it was probably not the type of lending that warranted authorisation on an unsecured basis. The reply would come as anticipated: "Mr B will guarantee it!" and Mr B would. Rumour had it that Mr B charged the account holder for his guarantee, but I do not know if that was the case. Occasionally if all other attempts to recover our lending had failed, it would be necessary to call upon Mr B to honour his guarantee. Thereafter the debt would always be repaid, not by Mr B, but by the account holder. What transpired between the debtor and Mr B following our call upon Mr B as the guarantor, and from whence came the funds that enabled the account holder to repay his debt, I never discovered, but it always worked.

On one occasion during a branch inspection, one of the younger inspectors remarked to his senior that the bank should evaluate its exposure under the guarantees given by Mr B. His guarantees were given not only to Stepney branch, but also to many other Barclays' branches, and to branches of other banks. It was a wise comment but it raised a question, and one that would have required the co-operation of all the major banks to answer. The main problem was the respect for the guarantor's right of confidentiality but many of the banks would not have wished to reveal the amount of their exposure. Even then, there were all the smaller non-clearing-banking houses, and perhaps some insurance companies who had also lent against Mr B's guarantees!

I believe that, some years after I had left Stepney, at the time of Mr Stern's bankruptcy, some effort was made to assess the amount of Mr B's liabilities as a guarantor. Nevertheless, I have not heard of a bank losing money as a result of accepting his guarantee as security.

It was the custom to entertain our customers from time to time, or to accept an invitation to lunch from a customer, but we never made these arrangements with the *frum*. This was not out of unfriendliness, but because of their strict culinary laws. These laws were so strict that even Blooms, the top of the London kosher restaurants, was not acceptable to them. They required a restaurant that would have a separate kitchen to cook meat and another one to cook fish, and preferably on different floors. The cutlery and crockery and all cooking utensils had to be washed in a different kitchen in order that knives and forks and dishes and pots and pans that had been used for meat were washed away from those that had been used for fish. Of course, all the other Mosaic laws about what could or could not be eaten were strictly applied. One rabbi once told me that when they flew to Jerusalem, members of the community insisted upon flying with BOAC (British Overseas Airways Corporation) as it then was. This was because they knew the Mr Silverstein who had the kosher contract with BOAC, but they did not trust El Al, the Israeli airline!

I went to Blooms on a couple of occasions and an amusing incident happened on one of them.

We had a Jewish customer who was in the knitwear trade, mainly making jerseys. He was not especially religious and probably attended a liberal synagogue, if any. His business was up and down, and occasionally he had to plead very hard with us in order to get his employees' wages paid on a

Friday lunch-time. At the time in question, things had gone rather well for him and he had bought a new Jaguar motor car, and he wanted to show it off. I was invited to lunch at Blooms, and we could have gone by bus, except for Mr R wishing to take me in his latest executive toy. It was a very nice car, and on the short journey to Aldgate, where Blooms then was, he regaled me with the story of his having taken Mrs R for a joy ride in the car on the previous Sunday, a hot, sunny day. They lived in Hertfordshire, and were driving around Buckinghamshire when Mrs R suddenly suggested that she would enjoy a Rossi's ice-cream. At that time Rossi was solely based at Southend-on-Sea (to the best of my knowledge) but on hearing his wife's wish, Mr R had immediately turned the car around and had headed at high speed for Southend, some fifty to sixty miles away! There was no M25 in those days, and on a hot Sunday afternoon the journey would have been rather tortuous, to say the least.

After a splendid meal we walked out into the car park. Unfortunately, as we did so a large Rolls Royce drove in and the driver hooted and drove up to me. It was one of my non-orthodox Jewish customers from Southend. He stopped and we exchanged a couple of words before he parked his car and went into the restaurant. I turned back to Mr R to see that all his ebullience had left him. His face was abject! He had come to realise that I knew people who drove Rolls Royces! He did not know that my friend from Southend ran a car-hire firm and all his vehicles were on lease. The Rolls Royce was the car that was hired out for weddings on Saturday afternoons.

One of the problems of doing business with the *frum* was that they were seldom available after lunch on a Friday. In the darkest days of winter, they would possibly not do any business because Shabbat (the Sabbath) commenced at sunset, when it was necessary for them to be indoors. This made life a little difficult at times. Out of courtesy, we never wrote business letters to them on a Friday, since they could not open them until sunset on the Saturday, and their Shabbat would be spoiled as they worried what might be in the letter until they were at liberty to open it.

I was taught not to hurry myself with applications for facilities that might be put to me on a Monday by the less orthodox Jewish customers. Having been to the synagogue on the Saturday, they would discuss business whilst the lengthy service was taking place. Often, I have been told, the cantor or the rabbi would have to reprimand such worshippers for talking too loud during the service. Having found out that Reuben had twice as much facility at the bank than himself, Solly would rush in to see his manager to arrange similar or greater facilities for himself on the Monday morning. The policy for the wise lending bank manager would be to leave the matter on ice until about the following Thursday. If he had really wanted it, the customer would have been telephoning or calling to see if it was granted. Otherwise it indicated that he had probably cooled down and had forgotten about the whole thing. Shortly after arriving at Stepney, I had put up a hurried application to Local Head Office one Monday. I had their approval to grant the facility by the Wednesday, and I had telephoned my customer to tell him, rather triumphantly, that he could have the facility. I was rather upset when he showed only mild interest, and seemed not to really remember what I was talking about. No, he did not think that he needed the money after all, but he was pleased to think that the bank would grant him a loan of that size if he should ever need it! I was very cross because of all the time I had wasted on his ungrateful behalf.

Clothing manufacturing, or the rag trade, as it was more commonly known, was our second largest customer base. Next to the rag-trade, in terms of numbers of customers, came market-traders, but we had one Stock Exchange quoted public limited customer namely, Time Products Limited. (This was in the days before the use of the name, Public Limited Company as a title.) That company was then the main distributor for the Russian Poljot watches that were widely advertised in the national press. Later the same watches were manufactured under the name of Seconda, and as such they are well-known and respected today. Amongst our customers there was also an umbrella manufacturing company, a smoked-salmon specialist company, a chain of ladies' hairdressers, many retail shops and a major car retailer and distributor. Several of our smaller customers had businesses in workshops and kitchens underneath the railway arches. One of these companies was renowned for its roll-mops and pickled cucumbers. There were a couple of builders and developers outside of the Jewish community. I enjoyed dealing with them, because, coming from Southend, such green-field building development financing had been meat and drink to me, especially at 45 Victoria Avenue.

The rag-trade customers kept us very busy. Some were complete manufacturers and made the garments from their own materials, and sold them under their own name. Others were supplied materials by the big retail houses, and had to cut, make, and trim, and were paid only for producing the finished goods to the large retail houses. To supplement their competitively priced returns from the retailers, the make-up customers relied upon "cabbage". It had been established in law that, if the cutter of the cloth could cut it skilfully and leave a surplus from the material supplied in order to make up a given number of garments, then that material could be legally retained by the making-up firm. It was emphasised that every garment manufactured for the retailer had to consist of the specified amount of cloth to make the garment exactly as specified, and there could be no skimping. The cutters were extremely adroit at cutting the cloth so that on a large order, often around two or three extra garments could be manufactured for the benefit of the manufacturer. One of our customers made up the famous Windsmoor coats for ladies. The favourite pattern was a red coat with a black nylon fur collar, and with a black herringbone design running the length of the coat from top to bottom. Any cabbage made by this firm was sold to the market-traders. The coats would be sold for less than half the price of a Windsmoor coat sold in Peter Robinson's or in C & A. The market-trader would point out what a bargain the purchaser was receiving. If the "cabbage" coat was made to the full specification of Windsmoor, as these coats sometimes were, then the purchaser really was getting a bargain, but such true bargains were few and far between.

Often the coat would have a lining of inferior quality to the real thing. Sometimes the material was cut to leave barely sufficient for the hem to be turned properly. In others, a close inspection would have revealed that on one or both of the sleeves the herring-bone pattern was running up instead of down. All these were manoeuvres by the manufacturer to get as much cabbage as possible.

Most Fridays, the owners of these small make-up companies would come for their wages but unless they had cheques with them from the John Lewis Partnership, Peter Robinson's, from C & A, or from other top retailers to pay into their company accounts, it was unlikely that they would receive the cash for their workers' wage packets. They would have been outside the buyer's office of their major retailer for probably the entire morning waiting for their cheques to be authorised for the accounts department to pay. If they did not receive payment before bank closing time, they had to rush to the bank and try their luck. Until the banks ended Saturday Opening in around 1968, if the bank would not help them on the Friday afternoon they would often have to go back to the retailer later on the Friday afternoon or on the Saturday morning to collect their cheque. Then they had to get to the bank by noon in order to cash their wages. I often felt sorry for them, but if the bank had given way and paid the wages on the Friday against promises, it would most likely have had cause to regret its action afterwards, and, in any event, it would have set a new precedent. To get round this problem, a group of sharp making-up manufacturers began to meet on Friday mornings in a pub where they formed a circle and each would write one, two or three cheques totalling a mutually agreed sum of say three hundred pounds. They would throw their cheques into the circle, and take out cheques drawn by their colleagues for a similar total value. They were careful not to make out the cheques for equal round amounts, and by each putting in three cheques, say, they could take out up to three cheques, each from a different drawer, to the value they themselves had put in. Armed with these cheques they could go to the branch where they banked and pay them in. They would try to claim their wages against these uncleared funds, and if the branch staff was not sufficiently astute to recognise that something irregular was afoot, they might have been successful. Such practice was known as cross-firing, or kite flying. The cunning idea was that, by the time the cheques were presented for payment, the drawer would have received his proper cheques in a more leisurely fashion from his retailer and having paid them in, the other cheques would be paid. This worked as long as the bank accepted the credits supplied by these cross-fired cheques without question. If the paying banker shrewdly returned the cheques with the answer, "Uncleared Effects", the whole house of cards collapsed, and any banker who had paid out cash against the cross-firing operation would be left holding the proverbial baby. We were always suspicious of accepting any cheque for the credit of these traders, that was not drawn by the recognised top clothing retailers. It was a common practice, however, for any manager of a branch on which the cheques were drawn, upon noticing such cheques, to telephone his opposite number at the other branch or bank in order to warn him that the cheques would be returned. The other manager would in his turn advise the other banks that he would not be paying the cheques drawn upon his branch. In this way all the cheques would be returned and no bank suffered any loss. It also showed the perpetrators that the banks knew what they were up to.

Most of our Jewish customers were the descendants of Jews who had arrived from Europe, especially from Russia and Poland. Many of their great-grandparents had arrived at Wapping Steps and had elected to set up their homes and businesses in the East End of London. They then threw themselves into all sorts of labour, working all the hours available in a day. They had worked for a pittance, especially in the rag-trade, where they won all the work away from the native English, who were not prepared to work so hard for so small a return. Eventually, many Jews were able to run business houses and they opened bank accounts. Stepney branch's predecessor won the lion's share of this new business. The original Stepney branch had been situated almost opposite the branch at 451 Commercial Road. The building was still there in my day, but was selling stationery, and was the place to go to purchase Jewish greeting cards, calendars and other specialised stationery.

The Jewish people were very loyal to anybody they considered to be sympathetic and helpful towards them, and some far-seeing managers of Stepney, predecessors to Joe, earned the undying loyalty of many descendants because of the assistance that had been given to their ancestors. One name in particular was always cropping up, a Mr Smith, who must have managed the branch in the early days. His name was legend to our Jewish customers, and, as a result, even though many had moved well away from the district, they insisted on leaving their accounts at Stepney.

When I arrived on the scene, immigrants from the Indian continent were doing to the Jewish businesses what the Jewish forefathers had done to the English. They would work in shifts with sewing machines for twenty-four hours a day in poor, very old accommodation, mostly flats of two or three floors above the run-down shops beneath them in the Commercial Road. Rumour had it that some forty people would be living and working in one apartment. One group worked as the other group slept, then, after a given period, they would change places. It was said that the beds never got cold! It was not only in the rag trade that the Asian immigrants competed with the Jews and the rest of the East End; they were also into the restaurant trade, delicatessens, and the small factories under the arches. Others were in on the fringes of the motor trade, especially in garages doing cheap repairs and even re-sprays. There was such a "garage" on a former bomb-site, right at the side of the Commercial Road, where they would re-spray vehicles amidst all the dust and diesel fumes emitted from the London buses and all the lorries, taxis and cars, as they plied their way to Gardners Corner. Often the traffic hardly moved when caught in solid traffic jams. The worst of these jams were usually caused by the opening of Tower Bridge to allow shipping to pass into the Pool of London, or to pass back down into the Thames' lower reaches. What David Fine, the driver of the Rolls Royce who had spoken to me outside Blooms, would have said about re-spraying vehicles under such conditions, I do not know. Just as I was leaving 45

Victoria Avenue, he had shown me his new paint-shop for re-spraying his hire-vehicles and other private cars. It had a low-bake oven situated in a dust-free zone.

Another of our accounts was known as X Dairy, and was run by an elderly lady. Many grocers' shops were called "dairy" in those days, and I had assumed that it was called X Dairy because it sold dairy produce as well as the usual groceries. To my surprise, I was to discover that, until only a year or two before my arrival in Stepney, there had been a farm alongside the road that led from opposite the branch down to Wapping, and past the famous Prospect of Whitby pub. Cows had been actually grazing alongside the Commercial Road! The land had since been taken over for a play area for children.

Occasionally, I had to go debt collecting, and I would take along our new chief clerk, Doug Hills. I had a friendlier relationship with Doug, as I did not sense that he was competing with me. We would don our long navy blue raincoats and try to look as much as possible like policemen. We would go around the back streets, often in the dark in the winter evenings. We had learned one good ploy, and that was to arrive before the husband or son, who owed us the money, had arrived home. If we could see the wife or the mother we had a better chance of getting our money back.

"Is Mr Y in, please?" we would ask.

"No. Why do you want him?" the lady would ask.

"I am afraid that it is a confidential matter," one of us would reply, "but please give him this business card." She would see the name of the bank on the card.

"Does he owe you money? How much?"

"We really cannot discuss it with anyone else. We shall call again when he is at home," and with that we would walk away. We had given her all the information that she needed. Invariably, the next day, the money would be paid in to clear the debt, usually by the lady.

On one occasion we had to visit a block of apartments in Cable Street. My heart sank as we made our way up the dark, threatening staircase, and I nearly turned back. We needed some money from a teenager. We reached the door and I knocked rather timidly. To my surprise a dark-haired gypsy-like woman, probably around forty, opened it, but she was the very woman whom I had seen on the television only a few nights previously. She was a musician who played the guitar. This was, of course, in the "swinging sixties" and the hippie movement was well established. She had been on a programme about helping the homeless in London. She received us courteously, and when we asked if the lad was there she took us to see him. The flat was a type of commune, with little furniture and the lad lay slumped in a corner, with a guitar lying nearby. He was obviously under the influence of some sort of narcotic and it was a hopeless case. We thanked the lady and left. The next morning we wrote off the relatively small debt.

1 *Above*: The old branch at 108 High Street, Southend-on-Sea: the branch was closed during the war with its business being combined with that of 24 High Street.

2 *Left*: 24 High Street, Southend-on-Sea: the branch where the author joined Barclays in 1945.

3 The Barclays Bank supervisors' course at Wimbledon, 1957 (author third from left, back row).

4 *Above*: The "Room" – in the old original building at 54 Lombard Street: Barclays' head office, see page 24.

5 *Below*: The Thames barge, *Kitty*, in the Barge Match, 1965 – author on extreme right.

6 *Opposite*: Ashridge Management College, November 1967 (arrow shows author in back row). The author was the only bank employee on the course; others came from major companies like Guinness, Rolls Royce, etc.

7 *Above*: Course leaders' group at Ashdown Park Management College in
1976 (author standing to extreme right).

8 *Below*: Retirement in 1989: the party was arranged by the author's under-
managers, past and present.

Chapter Eleven

Stepney: The General Way of Life

As I have indicated already, my tiny office was just an annex to the manager's office, with a communicating door between the two rooms. Instead of "Assistant Manager", the old-fashioned ornate gold leaf lettering on the window of my door read "Waiting Room". There had been many previous assistant managers at Stepney, most of whom had become senior managers in their own right, others had gone even higher to hold positions in Head Office. None of these had ever considered having this lettering altered. Perhaps, like me, they had anticipated the possibility of the early demolition of the building. When I arrived it was already condemned but, in any event, who was I to change an institution that had lasted for many years?

As they entered my room, my very *frum* customers, especially those who had taken to me, would put their blessing on my door-post. This was an orthodox tradition, and the front door of each house would have a *mezuzah* fastened to the top third of the door-post. A *mezuzah* was made from a piece of parchment on which was written two paragraphs of the *Shema*. The parchment would be rolled into a wooden or metal case and would then be fixed to the upper part of the right-hand door-post. It was recognised as an outward sign of God's presence in the building, and that the people living there were of the faith. The word, *Shema* literally translates as "Outward Sign". The custom was for orthodox visitors to touch this *mezuzah* by way of a blessing upon entering the house. I was always honoured by this gesture whenever I witnessed it being applied to my office door-post, despite the fact that there was no *mezuzah*. I write in the past tense, but, of course, this is an undying tradition.

One day, two very different people were shown into my room. They had not come by way of appointment, and I was just told that a Mr M and a Mr N wished to see me. They looked to be typical market-traders, one of about twenty-five, the other could have been ten years older, and they took their seats opposite me on the other side of my desk. I suspected that they would want to open an account, and probably to arrange an overdraft, and my attitude was guarded as I asked them what I could do for them. I was most surprised, even concerned at their response.

"If you don't mind me asking, guv," the older of the two replied, "how long have you been at this branch?"

The question aroused my curiosity. "About nine months," I replied. "Why do you want to know?"

"Well then," he went on, "you weren't here when it happened, but we've come in to see if we can get your help to get our things back from them robbing police at Arbour Square." Arbour Square was our nearest police station, and we had a good relationship with the local constabulary.

I looked puzzled. "When what happened, and what things?" I asked, completely bemused.

"Haven't you heard about the attempted robbery about two years ago?" he asked, and this time he was the one to look surprised.

"No," I replied truthfully. "What attempted robbery?"

"Well," he explained, "we came in here with a shooter—it weren't loaded, but he weren't to know that."

"Who wasn't?" I enquired, as I tried to feel for the location of the alarm button under my desktop, in case I should need it.

"The cashier. He was a tall chap and very fit. We didn't know that he had been in the police before. Well, he done no other than to leap over the counter showing no fear for the gun and came straight for us. So we scarpered, fast, and got away in our motor. He chased us and got a bloke in a car to follow us, and we got caught and was sent down for armed robbery but, as the gun weren't loaded, and as we never got nuffin', we got off light with two years each."

My eyes must have been popping out of my head, and I would have loved to have been able to press the alarm, but they had given me no reason to, up to that point. I was wishing that someone would come in with a message for me or that the telephone would ring, so that I would have had an excuse to leave the room.

This attempted robbery had occurred before security screens had been erected at branch counters and what he had told me was perfectly feasible.

"Well, guv," he continued, "we was taken to Arbour Square."

He had not explained how exactly they had been arrested, but I did not think it necessary to ask for precise details. I just wanted the interview to come to a close.

"At the station they made us empty our pockets and they took all our money, cigarette lighters and fags and everything that we had. They've never given them back to us!" he exclaimed indignantly.

I nearly suggested that perhaps the police had restored these items to their rightful owners, but thought better of it. "With respect," I said, "why have you come to us? Why don't you go to them?"

" Well," he said, "we've been there but they say that they took nuffin,' and had give us back the stuff what they took, but that's a lie. That geezer what chased and caught us was at the station when we was nicked and he saw what they took from us. If he would make a statement confirming what he saw, we could get our stuff back."

I was amazed at their effrontery. I said that the cashier was no longer with us, but that I would go outside to see if anybody knew where he now was. Once outside the door, I established that the story was true, so far as the attempted robbery was concerned, but, of course, no one knew anything about their possessions. W, who was the cashier at the time, had since left the bank, and his whereabouts were not known. I quickly appraised Joe of what was happening, but Joe was not in one of his good moods and he simply directed me to "get rid of them!" Easier said than done, I thought, but kept these thoughts to myself, and somewhat apprehensively I re-entered my room. They were still sitting there. I had hoped that they might have "scarpered" again, whilst I was out of the room.

"Sorry, gents," I uttered, "but W left the bank soon after the incident, and we have no idea where you can contact him." To my relief, they took it quite well.

"OK, thanks for trying. We did not really expect to get any help, but if he had still been here, who knows?" and with that they stood up and departed. I cannot express the relief that I had felt as they left the building.

What I learned afterwards was that everything had happened as they had stated. W, who was a strong rugby-playing young man in his late twenties, had leapt over the counter, as the robbers had run off. He had persuaded a customer who was just parking his car in Jamaica Street to follow them up the road. Because of this help and because of some smart work by W the arrest was made when the robbers came to a standstill in a traffic jam and W had managed to enlist the aid of a passing policeman to apprehend them. That is the story as it was told to me at the time. At the time, and for many years after, the bank had notices in its banking hall to the effect that the sum of one thousand pounds would be paid to any person whose actions resulted in the arrest and successful prosecution of any bank robber. The customer who had willingly agreed to take W in his successful bid to catch the robbers had expected to be paid his reward, but the bank that was usually quite generous in these matters had refused. This refusal was on the technical point that no money had been stolen, and therefore no money had been recovered as a result of this chase. The charge had been brought by the police and not by the bank! No wonder the customer was bitter about the matter. He was considering suing the bank, but did not wish to lose his case and any have to pay legal costs if his case should fail.

The late 1960s were the days of the gang wars involving the notorious Kray twins and their brother, and other gangs both north and south of the river. There were certain pubs that even Joe would not enter because they were known to be the haunts of the Krays. The most well-known of these pubs was The Blind Beggar in the Mile End Road, where an enemy of the gang was shot in front of numerous witnesses, none of whom could remember seeing anything, when questioned by the police later.

The East End pubs were usually cosy, friendly places, and Joe and Freddie Croasdell were well-known to the business types, mainly market-traders and other tradesmen from the area. If we went together into a pub, drinks would fly to us as if by magic from the moment we walked in through the door. Pubs were not usually known by their signboard names, but by the name or pseudonyms of their proprietors. The Exmouth Arms was always referred to as John Holland's, and it had been in the family for one hundred years. John, a chap in his early thirties was the successor to the pub when his father had died a year or two earlier, but his mother still ran the bar and served customers. Other pubs were similarly known. On my first Friday at Stepney, driven by a Mr Rich, one of our Polish customers, we had just picked up Freddie Crosdell from 140 Commercial Road and then we had called at George-the-Pole's, a large pub in a back street behind the London Hospital. Greetings were acknowledged as we entered, and, before I had taken a seat, drinks began to arrive on our table from all the other customers. I had never had vodka before that day, but that lunch-time I consumed six large vodkas, and would have had many more if I had not firmly refused to accept them despite Joe's protestations.

About the time that I was in Stepney, television brought out a very popular series called *The Star & Garter*. This show was all about entertainment in an East End pub and was really based upon the Old Iron Bridge pub. This pub was on the A13 near Plaistow, run by one of the stars of the show, Queenie Watts. The producer of the programme was Daniel Farsons who owned another pub on the Isle of Dogs called the Watermans Arms. I went to the Watermans Arms on two or three evenings. On one occasion, I took my wife and members of her family who were up from Cornwall on holiday. The entertainment was spectacular, and I have seldom enjoyed myself more, even at places where I have had to pay for admission. The pub was so well-known that many celebrities would go there incognito, and others would often give an impromptu performance. It became the "place to be seen". One evening, the master-of-ceremonies, the chap introducing the performers, came into the cloakroom at the same time as me. He started to refer to me as Johnny, and he asked if I was enjoying the evening. I enquired why he had called me Johnny, and he looked surprised, "You are Johnny Leach, aren't you?" I assured him that I was not, but he did not seem convinced that I was not the British table-tennis champion trying to remain anonymous for the evening.

One day the manager in charge of the standing order section of the EMI-dec computer centre came to Stepney branch and requested to see me. Most readers will be familiar with the expression "standing orders" in the banking context. Before the days of direct debits, standing orders were the authorities given to a bank to make regular payments from a bank account. Before computerisation, the writing of standing orders by hand or on a typewriter was a mammoth task, especially at the end of the month, when most standing orders were dated for payment. The advent of the computer took away much of this burden from the branches, who then had only to fill in forms showing clearly the account to be debited, the account to be credited, the date of payment, and the expiry date. Other than that, it was also necessary to advise the computer centre of any alterations to amounts to be paid as authorised by customer, and of any cancellations.

On this day, this manager came in to see me with a grave face. "I have to tell you that the standing orders of Stepney branch are by far the worst of all the branches on the computer! They are a complete shambles!"

The person who should have been organising a proper supply of information to the computer was, of course, the chief clerk, the one with whom I did not have a friendly relationship. That day it happened that he was away sick. It is fair to say that I had always felt that the administration of the branch routine was slack in the book-keeping area but as an assistant manager the situation was difficult. Sandwiched between the chief clerk and the manager, the responsibility for controlling the office lay with the chief clerk, and, if he needed to be criticised, it should have been by the manager. Joe had never involved himself in branch routine, and so it was down to me to investigate the problem, and, when I did, I discovered how appalling it was. One of our less able young girls had been given a desk in one of the empty upstairs offices and just told to "get on with it"! When I confronted her, she burst into tears, and it was obvious that she was far too immature to be left unsupervised with a job that called for simple but methodical approach and accuracy. What I also found were piles of unexecuted written authorities to open, to amend, and to cancel standing orders, all in heaps and mostly weeks old. As a consequence, new standing orders had not been commenced, and in many cases where they had been, there were already unexecuted instructions to amend or cancel them! There were so many that I just could not see how to start to clear it up.

The next evening, I called a meeting of all the senior staff in the Exmouth Arms before the pub began to fill up with its evening clientele, and I put the position to them. They were the supervisors, the securities clerks, the first and other senior cashiers. I stood them all a drink or two, and asked for volunteers to come forward to join me in a series of late evenings to clear up the awful mess. They were all frequently working late anyway, but I promised them that I would be generous with the overtime payments, for which I should need to do some explaining to Local Head Office on the monthly Overtime Return. By then overtime was being paid on a much fairer basis. Local Head Office would want to know why so many senior staff, who were paid top-rate overtime were working so late, but that was to be my problem. To my immense relief, I do not think that there was one who did not volunteer, and we started after normal work on the next evening. We organised ourselves into three parties. One party went through all the authorities and put them into separate piles – the new standing orders, the amendments and the cancellations. The second party then scrutinised the orders to see if the amendments or the cancellations referred to any of the new instructions, and quite a few did. The third party then prepared the forms for the bookroom machinists to process through the computer terminals on the next day. This took about four or five consecutive evenings of late working to about nine p.m. after which I stood a pint at the Exmouth Arms each evening to all those who were not in a hurry to get home. Thereafter, I made my weary way to Fenchurch Street Station to return home to Leigh-on-Sea, arriving home around midnight, only to have to get up to catch a train at about seven-thirty a.m. back to Stepney next morning.

Having ensured that the branch's standing orders were back in good shape, I was determined that they would not revert to the former mess. Therefore, I arranged for the standing orders to be put into the hands of one of our better younger staff, and had her all work verified by an excellent older woman, and we never looked back. Later, the manager of the Standing Orders section of EMI-dec kindly phoned to say that our branch was without doubt the *most efficient* on the computer. I had to thank all the excellent senior staff who had given me their unstinted backing, and who had done the job so well. They were a good bunch.

Whilst at Stepney I became an ex-officio member of the London Managers' Club. This club met annually in those days at the Grosvenor Hotel in the West End, but later, to save expense to the bank, which footed most of the bill, it became a triennial event. The Grosvenor was an enormous venue, and needed to be, because there were several hundred managers and assistant managers from all the London branches and head office departments who qualified to attend these sumptuous gatherings. Joe took me along to my first dinner in the spring of 1967. I remember gazing in wonder at the magnificence of the venue, and at all my managerial colleagues, and thinking, "I must be one of the youngest, if not *the* youngest member here!" I reflected upon this thought in 1988, when I attended the gathering shortly before my retirement. Chelmsford district had been absorbed partly into Cambridge Regional Office and partly into the newly created London and South Eastern Regional

Office ("Lesero" as it came to be known) and my branch, Basildon, had been enmeshed into the new region. This merger had the effect of qualifying the managers of the old Chelmsford district branches that had transferred into Lesero as members of the London Managers' Club. Consequently, when I attended in 1988, I reflected as I glanced around at all my colleagues, "I must be one of, if not *the* oldest member here!" Where had all those years in between gone? It had seemed such a short time.

We had some very amusing characters amongst our customers. There was one Jewish trader who made a point of making a din whenever he came into the branch. He would have some sort of small stick and he would bang this on the metal tray of a cashier's silver scales, and at the same time he would call out at the top of his voice, "Mr Cockle! Mr Cockle!" Don Cottle whose desk was at the back of the banking hall would pretend not to hear him but, after he had been called a number of times, he would shout back, "Go away, and stop making that row! We have respectable customers, and we do not want them to be offended by the likes of you!" or something similar. The customers in the banking hall, and the staff, all thought it great fun.

"Now come on Mr Cockle, I've got to talk business with you!"

After a given amount of this badinage, Don would go over in his droll way and would talk to him. It was usually all about nothing, but it made an amusing diversion in the day. On one particular day, the customer, let us call him Bernard, was even louder than normal. He stood in the banking hall, in an ebullient mood, banging on the metal scales and calling out to everybody, staff and customers alike, "At last! At last! I have paid off my overdraft after all these years! I have come to celebrate," and he produced an iced cake, a bottle of wine and some glasses and called upon everyone to join in his celebrations. The twist in the tale was that, in fact, he had miscalculated and his account was still in the red, at least for another couple of weeks.

A few doors away from the branch was our local newsagent from whom we bought the bank's daily and weekly papers and journals. The proprietor was one of those very pleasant but sober types, and he ran the business with the help of his wife, who was also a very friendly person. They say that dogs take after their masters; well, they had a big black old Labrador, and he too had the most placid of natures, as well as oozing common sense. Life for a dog, when living right on the Commercial Road, with no garden and with the constant roar of the traffic passing within a few feet of the shop door could not be ideal, but he made the most of it. He would curl up on the pavement just outside the shop, but he could not really rest for the need to keep one eye open to avoid the feet of passers-by, who, otherwise would trip over him. Occasionally, however, he would take himself off to do his rounds. Where he went or to whom, nobody, not even his master knew, but he would return after a couple of hours, and go back to sleep in his usual spot. To go on these excursions, however, he had to cross the Commercial Road. I have said that he was sensible, and so he was! Without anyone showing him how, he would always cross on the zebra crossing, and he did not wait to cross with people, but would amble across all alone. The remarkable thing was that all the traffic stopped for him as if he was a pedestrian. I have seen buses, lorries, taxis and private cars all stop while he crossed, and not all of them would have been as fussy for some old person. It was something that he had done for years, and frequent users of the Commercial Road all seemed to know him, and to look out for him.

We always advised our customers to avoid collecting wages or other large sums of cash at regular times on the same day of the week, but few would or could take this advice. It was very difficult for a small business to call for cash other than just before the wages had to be paid. The proprietors certainly would not want to keep a large sum in the factory, even if they had a safe, and they certainly would not wish to leave cash there overnight. They had little option, therefore, but to come on the same day and at the same time each week. Some would bring one or two heavily-built assistants from the factory or workshop to act as bodyguards, but not all had this option available, and so they tried to think of other ploys.

One day I was returning from my pie and a half-pint at the Exmouth Arms, when, as I reached Jamaica Street, I could see much activity on the other side of the road, outside the bank. Several of our male staff were huddled around a small blue van, which I recognised as belonging to one of our rag-trade customers. His was one of the smaller workshops, and he employed about a dozen people. As I approached the van, I saw blood on the pavement, and the customer was sitting on the driving seat of his van, with the door open and his feet on the pavement. His head and face were covered in blood, but to my astonishment he was laughing out loud. It turned out that some men had jumped upon him as he emerged from the bank carrying a blue copper bag containing his firm's wages. He had resisted them but they had hit him about the head and had knocked him to the ground. Only then had they been able to snatch his blue coin bag and run off. What had amused him was the fact they had taken only a couple of pounds of loose change, since he had stuffed all the bundles of notes into a specially manufactured lining in his anorak-type jacket. The police arrived and also an ambulance, and except for some of the staff giving witness statements about what little that they had seen of the raid, we left him in the hands of the authorities. The last I heard were his protestations against having to go to the hospital, since he had wanted to get back to his factory to pay his staff, and I believe that he got his way. He was a really tough little character, stocky, short, but full of grit.

Chapter Twelve

Stepney: More Characters
Ashridge Management College

Besides our large Jewish base, there was also quite a strong Roman Catholic community in the area. There was a big Catholic church nearby, for which we maintained some if not all of their banking accounts, and one morning a Roman Catholic priest had an appointment to see me. Although at 45 Victoria Avenue branch we had maintained an account for St Mary's Church, in Prittlewell, Southend-on-Sea, which was the main Anglican church in the borough, this was to be the first time that I had dealt with a Roman Catholic cleric with banking matters.

Fr J was shown into my office. He was a short, sturdy man dressed in his ankle-length black overcoat, with the usual black beretta on his head. I greeted him with the usual courtesies, which he returned in a pronounced Irish brogue, and then we got down to business.

"Now let me see, about the overdraft," he commenced. "It is nearly paid off, but I am going to need some more, but only for the short term. You see, I must pay the brewers, I have been holding back for far too long."

I looked at him in amazement and he then went on to explain how much he needed.

"As for repayments, well the football season is just about to start and I shall be starting up the weekly pools. The

Bingo takings will go up during the autumn and winter evenings. On top of that there are the weekly dances, which always help to increase the bar sales."

I could hardly believe my ears. Whereas I had previously discussed temporary financial assistance to the Anglican church, in anticipation of large Easter offerings in the collection boxes, I had not before come across a priest whose full-time duties for the local church was something akin to that of the entertainments manager of a Butlins' holiday camp! This very likeable little man was a minor priest in his church and he had been designated to organise all these events and to run the bar. Whether or not he ever officiated at any church service, I do not know.

About that time, Bishop Trevor Huddleston had returned from South Africa, and had taken up his appointment as Bishop of Stepney. I recall being introduced to him on one occasion when he had visited the branch, but I cannot recollect if we maintained any accounts for him, personally, or for the diocese. I just remember meeting this very affable man, who had received much press coverage for his stand against apartheid shortly before his arrival in the East End.

From time to time we would be served with a Garnishee Order to be attached to the banking account of one of our customers who owed money to a creditor whose patience had run thin. This was often not because the customer could not pay, but because there was a dispute with the creditor. The effect of a garnishee order was to freeze any available credit balance on any account held in the name of the debtor, until either the creditor's claim had been satisfied, or the court had resolved the matter.

We frequently had problems with small debts that were not big enough to take to court, but for which we wished not to give the debtor the satisfaction of realising that he or she had escaped without redress. During my time in Stepney I had made the acquaintance of a young solicitor whose firm was situated on the edge of the City, and whose speciality within his firm was debt-collecting and the pursuance of small debts, and he was very good at his job. At the time, we had as a customer a company of wholesale chemists, D Ys, which had been taken over by two brothers after their father had retired. Whilst in the father's hands the business had been well run, and we had valued the account. Shortly after they had taken over, the brothers had called upon Joe and had arranged unsecured overdraft facilities of five thousand pounds. The business was good and the facilities which were needed for day-to-day cash flow purposes were not unduly high in relation to the company's annual turnover. Before long, however, the account began to show all the signs of mismanagement, and the overdraft had been taken up to figures in excess of the agreed limit. What was worse, once the increased limit had been reached, the balance remained at that level and payments into the account ceased. The brothers were never available whenever we tried to speak to them by telephone. After a while it was evident that they had disappeared; as we were unable to trace them, it appeared that we had a bad debt on our hands. Fortunately, we had on our staff a very astute securities clerk, Ken Ring, who had observed a credit slip being paid into the account of an associate of the brothers D Y. The credit had come from the Dublin branch of a certain Irish bank. As a result, I enquired of my solicitor friend certain aspects of Irish law. Upon his advising me that my course was sound, I sent off one of the normal inter-bank status enquiries to the Irish Bank. It asked if, in the course of normal business, his new joint current account in the name of the De Ys was good for a specified sum of money, that sum being adequate to repay our debt. The answer was even better than I could have hoped for. Besides giving a good reply, it went further than is normal, stating that such funds were well within the *credit balances* held! I immediately telephoned the solicitor and asked him to serve a garnishee order upon the Irish bank. We waited a few anxious days to see the response. Almost a week passed before Joe received a telephone call from the Irish bank manager who was most irate. He called our action unethical. "Garnishee orders are not served by one bank upon another!" he maintained. "I will fight the order all the way!"

A few days later, however, we received not only a draft drawn upon the Irish bank sufficient to cover our overdraft and interest accrued and legal costs, but also a most threatening letter from the brothers, who maintained that they had always intended to repay us. If they had meant to be so open and above board, and had intended to repay the bank, why had they avoided all communication with us?

I have related this episode only because I think that it was a very rare occurrence for a bank to apply for a garnishee order to be served. It was far more usual for banks to be served with them.

When I had been at 45 Victoria Avenue branch, I had been asked by the local directors to do all that I could to help with recruitment of staff from the grammar schools and from the church-based schools who educated their pupils to General Certificate of Education standard. Consequently I had contacted the local education officer and the careers masters of these schools. By the time that I had left 45 Victoria Avenue, I had acquired a substantial knowledge of how to go about recruiting for the bank. In those days, banking faced strong competition from many other quarters for the best school-leavers who were not bound for the universities. Our main competitor for boys was Ford of Dagenham, and for the girls it was Marks and Spencer. Fords could offer the boys either company cars or the opportunity to acquire cars cheaply. Marks and Spencer offered the girls coiffeurs during working time and other perquisites. When recruiting, I would put before potential applicants what I could foresee as their career profiles, provided that they were prepared to work for promotion and would accept the necessity of qualifying themselves by sitting and passing the Institute exams. Nowadays, I wonder if any of them might consider suing me for negligent advice, for who could have foreseen what was to transpire in banking in the years from the early 1980s onwards?

When I arrived at Stepney, I had considered that recruitment was part of the job without referring to Local Head Office, and, once I had settled into the branch, I began to build up my contacts. There was a lady from the Tower Hamlets Education Office who was very helpful and she introduced me to a number of the local schools, to the headmasters and headmistresses and to the careers teachers. One of the first, if not *the* first comprehensive school had been opened at Tower Hamlets, and later the headmistress was to receive an award for her pioneering work in one of Her Majesty's honours lists. The lady from the Education Office, Mrs P, took me to Tower Hamlets school to meet the careers mistress and some pupils. We were invited to lunch, which was served in a guests' dining-room. The meal was cooked and served by pupils who joined us for the meal, and it was an excellent occasion in all respects, including the very sensible conversation. Often I would be invited to schools to talk or to hold discussions about careers with groups of pupils reaching school-leaving age. I was very impressed by their awareness of the world outside of school and for the need for them to try to shape a career rather than just to take a job. Unfortunately with the girls, all these splendid attitudes fell by the wayside after they had left school, and once they began courting seriously, so often with the wrong youths. It was at one of these schools careers meetings that some of the pupils had raised the contentious and sensitive subject of immigration, which was at its height. Most of the immigrants were black, mainly from the Caribbean, and from Jamaica in particular. Others were entering the country from the Indian continent. I had tried to steer away from anything that might have been considered racial, but one young girl said, "Why *should* they be allowed to come and take away all the jobs from us? We live here, and the jobs belong to us!" The girl who was speaking was of black African origin, whose parents had come from the Caribbean some fifteen years earlier. She had grown up in England, and she regarded herself, quite rightly, to be as much an English girl as any of her white colleagues. This incident certainly made me regard the racial problem in a new light.

Earlier in this chapter I have mentioned the Roman Catholic community. There were two Roman Catholic grammar schools in or near to Senrab Street, off the Commercial Road at the Gardners Corner end. On my first evening visit to one of these careers seminars, I was to meet Jean Temple, the assistant to Rooney Ede, the Women's Staff Assistant, at London Eastern Local Head Office. Later, when I was local head office manager of Chelmsford district, I was to persuade the Chelmsford district local directors to poach Jean from London Eastern district. Jean had come along to give me support and also to concentrate on enrolling more girls. London Eastern district had been so desperate to recruit women staff that Jean had only just returned from a recruitment tour of the Irish Republic.

The evenings at the Roman Catholic schools were a revelation. All the parents attended, and it seemed as if some edict had been sent from the Vatican to ensure a good turn-out. The school halls were always packed, and there would be representatives recruiting for the armed services, for other finance houses and industry but I was relieved to find that there were no representatives from other banks, and on my first visit I enquired why.

"You were the only bank to approach us," I was told.

Each representative was given about ten minutes to make an address and then, after taking questions from the audience of students and parents for about five minutes, the next careers representative had followed, and so on until they had all spoken. Afterwards, we all took up our "stands", consisting of wooden school desks in a classroom, and on which we had displayed and distributed our literature, whilst we answered questions from interested individuals personally. The evenings had usually ended at about nine p.m., when we were glad to make our weary journeys home, which in my case was some forty miles away by train. Thankfully on that first evening, Jean had given me a lift to the London terminal.

The turn-out on these evenings was always so excellent that I had never considered the effort to have been a waste of my time. The Roman Catholic schools have always impressed me with the devotion of their staff, most of whom were nuns, especially at the girls' schools, with Mothers Superior in charge.

Towards the end of my time at Stepney, I persuaded Mr Bolland, the local director with responsibility for recruitment, to take Mrs P, the local education officer and another lady from the council, with responsibility for local employment of school-leavers, together with Jean and myself to lunch. He took us to the Gallipoli, a Turkish restaurant in Old Broad Street. The Gallipoli was rather special, having been converted from a Turkish baths just before I had arrived at Stepney, and was situated at basement level, at the foot of a narrow stairway. As well as for its excellent cuisine, it was renowned for the special skills of its belly-dancer, Semra, who performed in the evenings. Its owner was a certain Mr Joe Murat, of whom I shall have more to write about in a later chapter.

On the day in question, the two ladies had joined me at Stepney branch, and I had taken them by taxi to Local Head Office at London Wall Buildings. On arrival we had been shown into Mr Bolland's room where Jean Temple, who was already known to the ladies, was also waiting. After a friendly greeting, and once introductions had been made, discussions about recruitment and the availability of potential entrants into banking ensued until about 12.50 p.m. when we had decided to take the short walk to the Gallipoli. Upon entering the lift one of the ladies had stated a preference to use the stairs. We had persuaded her that there were many stairs and that the lift was quite safe, but as the lift began to descend, it suddenly stopped between floors. We pushed the alarm bell but there seemed to be little reaction to our emergency for some time. Meanwhile, Mrs P who was claustrophobic had become quite distressed. After some ten minutes or more, voices were heard instructing us to, "Jump up and down!" Imagine giving such instructions to a local director with his lady guests!

Next, the voices informed us that they could do nothing to assist us until they could obtain help from the engineers working in Head Office at 54 Lombard Street. This help had eventually arrived after about another half an hour. Slowly the lift was lowered to the ground floor. Since the doors failed to open automatically, they had to be wrenched open with a jemmy. A remarkable sight met our eyes as the lift doors eventually parted and we emerged after having been stranded for over an hour. The whole of the wide spiral staircase was lined with people, most of whom were staff from London Eastern Local Head Office, but there were also others from London Northern Local Head Office, whose offices were on the top floor of the building, plus other sundry passers-by. They all gave a loud cheer as if we had surfaced after two or three weeks down a pit shaft following an accident. With the ladies apparently recovered from their ordeal, we then proceeded quickly to the Gallipoli for our lunch.

Referring back to the Roman Catholic school in Senrab Street, you will have perhaps noticed the Senrab is the reverse spelling of Barnes. Barnes Street and Senrab Street were close to each other. Some other examples were pointed out to me how, in many areas of the East End, the town planners of yesteryear had run out of street names and, in order to solve the problem, they had simply reversed the name of an adjacent street or road.

One of the most controversial persons to bank with us was the dockers' local trades' union leader, Jack Dash. The dockers were at their most militant around that time, and, as I have mentioned, I met many of them most days in the Exmouth Arms during my lunch-breaks. I must say that they were a most friendly bunch, and there were never any altercations, but friendly banter would be exchanged on occasions. It was not our place to argue with them, although sometimes we would suggest that they were taking great risks with their livelihood, because of all their strikes. Often they would come out in sympathy with some cause that was totally unrelated to stevedoring. On one occasion they all marched up Whitehall and around the West End, carrying banners in support of an issue that was really none of their business.

"It was marvellous," one of them was saying in the Exmouth Arms on the following day, "work was stopped on twenty-eight ships!"

"You will kill the docks with all these strikes!" we had replied, but even we had not really believed what we said, because the London Docks were then the hub of the empire, or what remained of it. The jobs in the docks had been handed down through the families for many, many years, and it looked as if this pattern was set to continue forever. Little had we realised how close our prophecies were to being fulfilled. Container ships and greater use of airfreight were still in the future, but time was fast running out.

I had been rather apprehensive when the name of Jack Dash had been entered on my appointment list one day. All I knew of him was the fiery-tongued orator who had appeared on the television screen condemning the capitalists and appealing to his brother workers to stand up against the bosses for the benefit of the working-classes. I had not been prepared for the mild-mannered rather gentle man who had been shown into my room. By the time he had left me, I had quite warmed to him as a person, but, of course, no politics of any kind had entered our conversation.

Every so often local head offices and certain of the branches in their districts were subjected to Directors' Inspections. A team would be created which would consist of local directors from various districts, one of them being nominated as the leader. This team would inspect the districts that had been designated to them. First, they would visit the local head offices and look through the major advances, and talk to the local directors and to the local head office staff. Then they would do much the same in the branches which they had selected to visit within these districts. In 1967 London Eastern district was inspected by a the team that was led by a local director from Reading district.

I have already alluded to the fact that the bank was having difficulty in recruiting staff. This was mainly because of the competitive salaries on offer to staff particularly from the financial and other business houses in the City; they would often poach bank staff for their acquired skills, after the banks had met the cost of training them. Realising that I had only recently come from a country district in the home counties, this local director remarked to me about the ratio of male staff to female in London compared with districts such as Reading and Chelmsford. In Stepney, the ratio was about sixty-forty, men to women, but in the country districts close to London the ratio was often as low as thirty men to seventy women. Indeed, in Chelmsford district at the Thorpe Bay branch, which had a lady manager, there was, at one period, a staff consisting of seven women and one man. It was thought to be necessary to maintain at least one man on the staff for security reasons. Incidentally, Dorothy

Hawken, the lady manager at Thorpe Bay, was only the fourth such appointment in Barclays at that time. Dorothy had been one of the securities clerks when I had been appointed assistant manager at 45 Victoria Avenue in 1965. The main reason for this discrepancy in the ratio of men to women between London and the country branches was, I believe, because of the London Allowance, which was paid to London-based staff. People employed in London received this allowance which was usually sufficient to cover the cost of travelling with, perhaps, a little to spare. In the country, however, especially in the days when car ownership was restricted to those higher paid staff who could afford to own a car, travelling to country branches could be time-consuming and costly. Therefore, to those who lived close to a reasonable rail service, working in London was much more attractive.

I once made myself very unpopular at a Staff Association meeting in London Eastern district when I had the temerity to make this point. There were many anomalies throughout the country where, in certain large conurbations, Large Town Allowance was paid in lieu of London Allowance. Staff would be paid the allowance for travelling *into* the large town from the country, but those travelling *from* the large town to the country would not be, and yet the fares were the same. The Staff Association was a milder version of the National Union of Bank Employees (NUBE), and related only to Barclays, whereas the NUBE covered all banks. It was in the bank's interests to foster the Staff Association, to whose complaints and observations it usually seemed to react more sympathetically than to those of NUBE. I believe that it was really a deliberate case of "divide and rule" because, acting separately, the two staff representative bodies were far less effective, and, quite frequently they outwardly disagreed with each other, much to the bank's benefit.

Over the years many efforts were made to bring the two staff bodies together so that they could talk to the bank with one voice, but these efforts came to nothing during my time in the bank. To get bank employees to act together on an industrial issue, especially to strike or even to work-to-rule was virtually impossible. Situations and circumstances varied so much from district to district. What was a cause for concern in one part of the country was not seen to be a problem in another. There was also a close paternalistic relationship between the local directors and the district staff, most of whom were afraid of the consequences of being seen to be trouble-makers. They did not anticipate dismissal or a public reprimand, but they feared that they would miss out on advancement in their careers, since their superiors need give no reasons.

In November 1967 I was sent on a management course to Ashridge Management College, near Berkhampstead, a few miles north of London. Ashridge is a magnificent building standing in acres of ground that include vast areas of woodland in which deer roam freely, and large ornamental ponds. We were warned about the deer upon arrival. It was the rutting season, and the stags could be quite dangerous. I paid particular attention to this as I was still playing rugby football for the school's Old Boys side, and was training hard at the advanced age of thirty-seven in order to retain a first or second team place out of the five teams that the club fielded. Nearly every morning, at around six a.m., for the four weeks that I was at Ashridge, I went for a half-hour run around these marvellous grounds, even in the snow of that cold November in 1967. Sometimes I had company, but most often I ran by myself.

I was the only bank officer on the course of about fifty students. Most of the others came from the larger companies such as Rolls Royce Aeroengines, ICI, Guinness, and Truman Hanbury and Buxton, the brewers, and many others. A couple of students had sent themselves on the course from their self-owned companies. It was hard work, as we started at eight a.m. and finished at eight p.m. We worked through the weekends except for the middle weekend, when we were sent home on the Friday afternoon to return on the following Monday morning.

The building had been completed in about three stages over the centuries, but it had all been constructed to a high and quite beautiful standard. There were impressive stone stairways, and halls and several ceilings depicted classical scenes that had been painted by prominent artists. We were told that the building was often used by film-makers either in part or as a whole. Whilst we were there we frequently saw models posing in various areas, most often by the ornate main staircase. Tales of resident ghosts abounded, but I cannot recollect any having been seen by any students on our course.

There was a principal and a couple of lecturers on the permanent staff, but most of our lectures were given by captains of industry; politicians, or professors who were called in for a particular subject. In my opinion, the principal was rather pompous, to the point of appearing rather a charlatan to me.

The course covered many aspects of business management, and introduced us into the world of Management Accountancy, the brainchild of the famous (or infamous, according to one's point of view) Peter Drucker. It was one of the key subjects of his books, which had attracted world-wide acclaim. The management was quite astute, however, and had proved it when, at the drop of a hat, it had completely re-scheduled the course to take in the devaluation of the pound sterling. This announcement was contained in Harold Wilson's notorious "pound-in-your-pocket" speech.

Being the only bank officer on the course, I felt as if I was more of a spectator than a participant. All this budgeting and profit planning may well be of interest to industry. Except for the top echelons of the bank, i.e. the only people to know the *true* profits made by the bank, I could not see how it could apply to a branch manager who had no real control of his resources. All staff were designated to the branches by the staff department of Head Office, or from the local head office. The amounts paid to the staff were not under the control of a branch manager; neither did he have any right to sack inefficient staff. If a branch manager wished to get rid of a member of staff, who in his opinion was useless, the worst thing that he could do would be to give that staff member a bad report. Local head offices would not wish to send an inefficient member from one branch to another and, in those days, they would not wish to sack staff for two reasons. First, the bank sacked its staff only for reasons of dishonesty, seldom were staff dismissed for inefficiency. Secondly, they would not have wanted to engage in an agonising tussle with the NUBE or with the Staff Association, both of which bodies were vigorous in defending their members.

Policy was always dictated down from Head Office, through the local head offices to the branches, and therefore a branch manager could not go against the bank's overall policy to suit his local needs. If the bank were to decide to curtail all personal lending, then the branch manager had to concur. At one time the bank decided to stop lending to personal customers to purchase their homes under the old Home Loan Scheme, before the days of bank mortgages. This ruling badly affected branches that had a predominance of personal customers, compared with branches in industrial areas. What could be charged for lending to customers was completely outside of the branch manager's control, since most lending was linked to the Bank Rate, set by the Bank of England, and, later, to individual banks' own Base Rates. All banking hours were fixed by Head Office. For all these reasons, and for many others, I could not foresee management accounting applying to the running of the branches. The banks did bring it in but in my opinion it was always a costly sham, of very little true worth. It was really intended to get the less well-organised managers to look more carefully at the way they conducted the business in their branches. To the efficient branch manager it was a time-wasting and ineffective chore.

The main benefit that a bank manager could get from studying management accountancy was to understand how his corporate customers were running their businesses. I quite believed in management accounting, and, in fact, I was later to become a Group Leader (Instructor) on the subject on the managers' courses at the bank's own management college at Ashdown Park, in the Ashdown Forest. Management accounting was fine, but lending managers would have been advised to remember the old adage, "First, know your customer!" Many of our Stepney customers would ask to borrow, say, five thousand pounds for their business. After a lengthy discussion, however, they would agree to accept two thousand five hundred pounds, which was all that they had really needed. They would have asked for the five thousand pounds, in anticipation of being talked down to a lower figure. It was the way that business was done. However, if they had asked for five thousand pounds and had then been asked to bring projections to prove that they needed the whole five thousand pounds, they would have had no trouble in producing them. I can hear in my mind's ear the conversation that would have taken place, first. "So, Mr Sherringham, you want me to produce figures to prove that I need five thousand pounds? Of course, you shall have them!" and within a couple of days they would have been on my desk. Then I would have had a harder task to reduce the figure to a more realistic sum. Such customers seldom had reasons for wanting to borrow specific amounts of money. They lived by doing deals, and they would want a bit here and a bit there to enable them to keep going until one of their other deals had paid off. We were always repaid eventually, but in the meantime we were able to charge high commissions and interest rates, and few objected as long as they could come back another time. The Jewish community, whether the orthodox or otherwise, seldom let their bank manager down, because he was the life-blood of their business deals. They may not have kept strictly to a repayment plan, and in many cases we would have been surprised if they had. Sometimes one would become known to be a bad lot, but the bank was always warned by the rest of the community to avoid him, and it would be a "him", for few ladies were in that kind of business. I am, of course, referring to the smaller one-man affairs. The larger companies soon came to employ either their in-house financial directors or outside firms of chartered or incorporated accountants to draw up their projections. Even so, such figures needed careful scrutiny, and if outside influences were to drive even the most carefully plotted targets off course, as they so often did, then a feasible escape route had to be available, or gilt-edged security taken.

Most of the lectures at Ashridge were to the whole class and were held in the main hall. They were upon varying subjects from advertising and its benefits, to political lectures on the economic climate. We also spent much of each day split into syndicates, often with a project to complete, and the syndicates would be in competition with each other. Syndicates comprised some eight students each, and the students took turns to chair the meetings on a rotary basis for each topic. In order to complete the task and to be ready for the presentation on the following morning, syndicates often felt it necessary to continue working after supper and the midnight oil was frequently burned. There were recreation facilities available, mainly tennis and golf, and my jogging, but there was really little time for such activities.

At the end of the course we were split into two teams participating in the financial equivalent of military war games. It seemed to be intentional that the representatives of Guinness were put into one team, and those from Truman Hanbury and Buxton were in the other. The game lasted for the entire last two working days of the course, and each team was supplied with its own barrel of beer from each of the brewers, although I am quite sure that each team sampled some of the wares of their opponents.

After the course, we all went back to our own businesses. About twelve months later we were called back for a long weekend on a feed-back and a refresher course. Shortly after that, a bankrupt Rolls Royce had to be bailed out by the Edward Heath administration.

Chapter Thirteen

Joe Holmes

Of the many characters that I have met in my lifetime, none can compare with the late Joe Holmes. Anyone who ever met him would smile just at the mention of his name. They all knew Joe. He was one of those larger-than-life types who influence the lives of all who come into contact with them. Joe had a powerful will, and once in his clutches, it was hard to break away. Strong and even powerful men in the bank have crossed the street to avoid him, not because they disliked him, but because they could not trust themselves once he had taken charge. The reader will recall that, when I had been called to see the general managers upon my appointment to Stepney as assistant manager, a branch manager, up for promotion to a larger branch on the same day, had advised me to take my "drinking boots" with me to Stepney! The advice was to prove to be sound.

Joe was a manic-depressive, and he was either on a high or a low, but he seemed to save his bad temper for the office because, when he was socialising, he was a gentleman of the greatest charm. The trouble was his addiction to alcohol. He was not an alcoholic in the recognised sense of the word, but he would drink socially all day and all night if he had company, and that was what his companions feared most. By saying "drinking all night" I do not exaggerate, as I shall recount. His colleagues and friends who had become caught up with him at some lunch or other, and who, very unwisely, had agreed to go off to one of his drinking clubs in the afternoon, would have been extremely lucky to have caught any train before the last one home, and many had often missed that. Many a long and expensive ride in a taxi had been taken after midnight by gentlemen who had to find good explanations to give to their irate spouses when they had eventually arrived home in the small hours. Many a wife thought of Joe in the same way that they might have considered a seductive female who was attracting the attention of their husbands, and keeping them out late. "Joe Holmes! Urgh!" most of them would growl at the mention of his name, but when they met him socially, however, they would become coy at his most gentlemanly greeting, and would call him a "naughty man!"

On my first Friday at Stepney, I met a Mr Rich, who was a semi-orthodox Polish Jew, semi-orthodox in that he was not bearded, but he kept most of the traditions of the orthodox. I never really got to know the rather complicated Polish first name of Mr Rich, but he was a great friend of Joe. It had been Mr Rich, who on my first Friday at Stepney had accompanied us to George the Pole's pub, as I have related earlier. In his business he had acted as a trade representative in Poland, both for his own rag-trade business and for any exporters or importers who wanted to do deals with the Poles. He travelled to Poland, mostly to Warsaw weekly, but was always back in time for Shabbat on a Friday. He would call at the bank to see Joe every Friday lunch-time, at about noon. On his way to the bank, Mr Rich would call into Strongwaters, a restaurant-come-take-away for Jewish food, to purchase salt-beef sandwiches, latkes (deep-fried potato cakes), and pickled cucumbers. He always went to Strongwaters, not Blooms, as Strongwaters' latkes were "much nicer" and, having tried both, I would have agreed with him. Sadly neither of these once excellent restaurants remains open, today.

Each Friday he would be called into Joe's room with his paper-bag, full of steaming food, and lay it on Joe's desk, together with a bottle of vodka. Now the vodka in this bottle would not be the ordinary everyday vodka such as would have been purchased in the off-licences, but had been brought back from Poland by Mr Rich on his latest trip. The strength was the equivalent of about one hundred and fifty per cent proof, compared to the strongest of British vodka at about forty per cent proof. Joe's desk was very old-fashioned and the surface was covered with a plate-glass top. The central-heating in Joe's room was very inefficient, but on a winter's day, I have seen a spoonful of this vodka poured on to the cold glass surface and go up in a bright puff of flame as a match was applied. Often I have tried to ignite the brandy poured over our Christmas puddings at home, but without success unless the brandy has first been heated in a saucepan. There was no such problem with this vodka, which was considered to be almost one hundred per cent wood-alcohol. The vodkas that he brought us were not always just the plain spirit, but there were many delightful varieties usually blended with berries, but my favourite was the cherry-flavoured.

As Mr Rich arrived, I and one other member of the staff would be called into Joe's room not only to join in the feast, but, also to make up a foursome at dominoes, Joe's favourite game. I came to enjoy these Friday lunch-times, as the salt-beef sandwiches and latkes were delicious, and so were the pickled cucumbers. It was a job to ensure that not too much vodka was imbibed. At about one p.m. I would tear myself away and get back to work.

Dominoes figured very prominently in our routine at Stepney. I had never played the game before, but had needed to learn not only the rules, but also the skills, very fast. On one of their earlier "benders", Joe Holmes and Fred Croasdell had somehow acquired a metal figurine of a cockerel, the advertising symbol, or what we would now call the "logo" of Courage's brewery. They had either had it given to them, or they had purloined it with the acquiescence of a barman who had obligingly looked the other way. By whatever means they had acquired it, they looked upon it as their trophy. It had been agreed between them that it should be played for at "John Holland's" i.e. the Exmouth Arms, at lunch-time on the Monday following pay-day in order to decide which of them should have it adorning his office for that month. Pay-day in the bank was on the twenty-third of each month, except when the twenty-third fell on a weekend, when an adjustment would be made by paying the staff either on the Thursday prior to the twenty-third or on the Monday following. The monthly match was between Joe and his assistant manager, against Freddie and his chief clerk at 140 Commercial Road. Freddie's chief clerk, Bernard, and I both dreaded these matches, as neither Joe nor Freddie liked to lose, but Joe could turn positively unfriendly in defeat, especially if his assistant manager had played carelessly. We would sit in the saloon bar of the Exmouth Arms at a polished wooden table for four, with our pies and our glasses of ale, and our dominoes spread out before us. The monthly match was well-known to the frequenters of the pub and they would gather round to watch, frequently giving unhelpful advice! On other occasions, one or two of the bystanders or some unsuspecting customer who was visiting Joe at the branch would be lured into a game. It was usually played for money, but only for ha'pence, and nobody could lose much, and it was quite enjoyable.

Joe introduced several variations of the game, one of which was known as "Thirty-up". It was based upon low scoring, and once a player's score exceeded thirty, he was out. However, under a certain rule, players could buy themselves back into the game for a given number of times. The winner was the last player left with a score below thirty. I remember once reading a short story by one of my favourite humorists, P G Wodehouse, where a rather crooked noble lord would introduce those whom he intended to fleece to a card game called "Persian Monarchs". None of the victims had ever heard of the game before. The rules appeared to be complicated and only fully understood by the noble lord who always won, and many doubting losers suspected that he made them up as the game progressed. Many other players and I felt the same way about Joe's variations on the game of dominoes. On one memorable occasion when the branch was being inspected, the senior inspector of the team brought a couple of his assistants over for a lunch-time sandwich and a pint at the Exmouth Arms. One of the advantages of "Thirty-up" was that it could be played by more than four players, probably using two sets of dominoes.

The inspectors were invited to join in, and accepted. With players frequently "buying themselves in", the game went on for what seemed to be an age. Eventually, one of the younger inspectors stood up and made a somewhat unwise statement.

"Sir," he said to his boss, "this game cannot possibly be finished. There is something crooked about it!" There was an embarrassed hush.

"Sit down and get on with it!" replied the senior inspector, who knew Joe very well. The lad sat down and the game proceeded to its eventual conclusion and we all returned to the branch. I am sure, however, that the young inspector still retained his doubts about how genuine was Joe's version of the game of "Thirty-up"!

There were some other memorable occasions when dominoes were played in the branch over a glass or two. One day Mr Pelley, one of my local directors at Chelmsford, visited us. He had cause to go to Head Office, and kindly arranged to call in to see me whilst in London. Mr Pelley was a rising star and was destined later to become the personal assistant to the chairman of the bank, a very senior position. I believe that Mr Pelley's path had crossed with Joe's in a London West End branch on their respective ways up the ladder, because Mr Pelley seemed to know all about Joe and his habits. At the time I had a suspicion that he had wanted to see Joe as much as he had wished to see me. Anyway we all enjoyed a very convivial time, and I found myself drinking Scotch and playing dominoes with a person whom only a short time before I had regarded with something amounting to reverence.

On another occasion, Ken Williams, who had been my manager when I had left 45 Victoria Avenue, was to be promoted to manage of one of the bank's largest branches, Bank Plain, Norwich. Contrary to much general belief, most of the bank's largest branches were outside London. Many had been the head offices of the old partnerships which had over the years amalgamated to create Barclays Bank Limited. These country-based head offices had usually been set in the market towns, and had served the farmers and business from miles around.

On this day, Ken was due at Head Office to have his new appointment confirmed by the general managers at three p.m. Unwisely, as it turns out, he arrived at about twelve-thirty p.m. in order see me and to have a bite of lunch. Joe would not allow this, but sent out for sandwiches and then called us both into his room to play dominoes in an atmosphere of great joviality, until we suddenly realised that not only was time getting on, but that Ken was becoming rather the worse for wear! We had to bundle him into a taxi and send him on his way. Unfortunately, it was one of those days when the Commercial Road was snarled up and the traffic was just not moving. The taxi driver had to go on a circuitous route for the otherwise very short journey to Lombard Street. Ken later recalled to me how he had arrived in a lather and quite tottery on his feet, and a few minutes late for the most important interview of his life! He could not have made too bad impression because he got the job and a year or two later he was promoted to be a local director of Norwich district. All's well that ends well!

Joe was always at his best at a farewell party for a member of staff who was leaving the branch. This party would be held in the Exmouth Arms at the end of the day. "One each apiece all round!" was a familiar call when Joe was around in any pub, and so it would be. Often Freddie Croasdell would join us, and as the party got into full swing, Joe would call for a song. He, like many of the Stepney staff, were avid West Ham United supporters and he would lead a chorus of "I'm Forever Blowing Bubbles", the equivalent to the national anthem so far as West Ham supporters were concerned. His other speciality was "Knees Up Mother Brown" accompanied by all the actions. All the rest of the pub's customers loved these evenings and would join in, both receiving and buying drinks. Joe had made Barclays in Stepney a really integral part of the local community. Somehow he had still managed to retain his dignity. At the end of the evening Freddie would slip away with me to the station to catch a reasonably early train home. The alternative would have meant him being dragged around Joe's drinking haunts, and having to make explanations to Doris, his wife, on his arrival home well after midnight.

Joe had one especial customer friend, Maurice Gold, who was generally known as "Morrie". Morrie owned a chain of ladies hairdressers' shops, which since his retirement were being run by his son. Morrie would arrive at the branch around midday in his large expensive motor car, a Jaguar, or a Daimler, no less. He would drive himself, because drink-driving was not of such concern as it is today. After a chat over a couple of Scotches, he would take Joe off to the Windmill, a drinking club at Bermondsey, which was also owned by Joe Murat, the proprietor of the Gallipoli. Joe Murat's cousin, Ali Murat, ran the Windmill. One thing that never bothered Morrie was a parking ticket. Parking meters and traffic wardens had just been introduced to London together with the now familiar double-yellow lines. The fine for parking on double-yellow lines was two pounds, which seemed to be a lot of money to ordinary people in those days, but to Morrie it was just a fair price to pay in order to park close to the place that he wanted to visit. The tickets were sent to his son for the fines to be paid out of the hairdressing business. Therefore he and Joe went on their joyful way, parking as when and where it pleased them, even in the West End, but their usual destination was the Windmill in Bermondsey. There they would be welcomed with open arms by the host. Whether Ali was really as pleased to see them as he made out, I do not know. He had on frequent occasions been called from his bed by Joe and a gang of friends who had decided that they had wanted some more to drink and something to eat at midnight or even after.

Morrie and Joe would have more drinks and then take wine with their sumptuous lunch before joining the other diners in the bar after the meal. These other diners would often be businessmen with their attractive secretaries. Later in the afternoon, Morrie would take his leave and drive to his home in Surrey.

Meanwhile I would be working away in the office, and by five-thirty p.m. the cash reserve would have been put away, and the day's work and the remittances would have been agreed. Usually, whilst signing the post, I would receive a telephone call from Joe.

"Now Denis, are you busy? Is everything all right?" he would ask. In the early days I would reply that I was not busy and that everything was fine, but, once I had become familiar with the routine, I changed my response. "No, I am up to my eyes! Everything is in a mess! The remittances are wrong and we cannot agree the day's work," I would lie. He knew that I was joking.

" Well, I am sure that you are well in control!" Joe would reply. "Get a taxi, and bring my coat, my bowler, my gloves, my rolled umbrella and *The Times*, and join me in the Windmill."

"All right, but I can't promise how long I shall be!" and with that I would end the conversation and replace the receiver.

To request a taxi to come to Stepney branch was a laugh. The taxi drivers avoided Joe like the plague for reasons yet to be explained. The only chance of getting a taxi would be to go out into the Commercial Road and thumb down some unsuspecting driver from the West End. It was just as quick to get a number fifteen bus from across the road to the Minories, and from there take another bus to Bermondsey, which would stop just across the road from the Windmill, and this was my usual method.

Whenever I entered the club, there would be Joe holding court to all the company. Many of the more regular diners knew Joe quite well, and thought him to be a great entertainer, as well as enjoying his generosity when he frequently sent to the bar for "One each apiece all round!"

"Now here is Denis!" he would announce, as I entered. "Denis, like all bank clerks, is the salt of the earth!" and I would receive a salutation from the amused drinkers. "However," Joe would continue, "Denis is not one of us! He will not stay and drink with us. He is under the thumb, and he will be going home!"

"Quite right, I shall!" I would reply, and after having one drink to be sociable, I would beat a hasty retreat on the bus to Fenchurch Street station to catch the train home, at about seven p.m.

Joe was very disappointed in me for never once joining him for the rest of the evening, as had been the custom of

146

my predecessor, but I knew that the "rest of the evening" would have become *all night!*

The reason that Joe had such a bad name with the taxi drivers was that, once he had hailed one, he would not pay him off until he had finished with him. For example, assuming that he had gone off with Morrie to the Windmill at lunch-time, Joe would probably have taken a cab from the Windmill at about seven p.m. He would head for the Gallipoli, where he might stay until midnight, before going to Joe Murat's nightclub, L'hirondelle, which was situated close to St James' Park, in the West End. On the light summer mornings he would go to feed the ducks on the lake in St James' Park at about four-thirty a.m. and then, at long last, he would allow the cabby to take him to his home at Ashtead, near Epsom in Surrey. For all that time he would have kept the cabby on the meter! On arriving home at about five-thirty a.m. he would meet his wife, Dorothy, who would be on her way for early morning mass at the local church. Dorothy was not only a very devout churchgoer, but I think that she must also have been a saint. They had met when they were both working in Shoreditch branch before the war. Well, Joe would raise his hat to Dorothy as they passed on the garden path. He would then take the cabby into the kitchen and give him breakfast of bacon and eggs and tea or coffee, and only then would he pay the poor fellow and let him go. On other occasions, if a taxi driver were to ask Joe directions to a destination, Joe would try to deduct money from the fare, in return for supplying the cabbie with "the Knowledge". So now, perhaps it can be understood why the cabbies avoided him, and why they would never come to the branch if called by telephone. I am referring to the ordinary London black cabs, because, to the best of my recollection, mini-cabs were not operating or were in their infancy in the late 1960s. Having disposed of the cabbie, Joe would have a nap on the sofa before washing, shaving and attending to his attire, and then he would catch the train back to Stepney, via London Bridge to be back in his office shortly after nine a.m. It would be quite likely that, after doing a brilliant morning's work, he would be off again at midday for a repeat performance of the day before! He was sixty in 1969, and how he could carry on this lifestyle at his age, without suffering for it, I just do not know. He would go on these escapades at least four times a week, and the stories of his antics, as told by those who were unlucky enough to be towed along in his wake, are legion.

After one such night, he and another colleague who had been out with him headed for Waterloo to catch their respective last trains. They were both very tipsy and having insisted on seeing the other fellow to his train, Joe took the wrong train and, instead of going to Ashtead, had arrived at a terminus that may have been Slough. This was the outcome of having travelled in the opposite direction to that in which he had wished to go. There was no train back to Waterloo until about five a.m. It was raining and he could not remain on the station, which was to be locked overnight. Having no option, Joe entered one of the old red telephone boxes, piled up the several sections of the London telephone directory on the floor and sat on them with his rolled umbrella between his knees and had an uncomfortable night. He must have dozed off because the next he knew he was being woken by a policeman. In those far-off days, constables were far more understanding of City gents who had taken a few too many, and this one had merely escorted Joe to the station which had opened by then, and seen him on to his train. Joe returned home, cleaned himself up and came into the office, as if nothing untoward had occurred. The only thing different about him was that he had a cut above his eye, which he claimed had been caused when he had fallen and smashed his spectacles. There were some cynics who thought that he may have said the wrong thing to the wrong chap in a pub! We shall never really know.

On another occasion Joe and Freddie had gone to some special party, probably the retirement party of a mutual colleague. FG, the chief clerk of Stepney, who lived in Thorpe Bay, had gone with them. After the party, they had to go to one of their haunts, possibly the Gallipoli or L'hirondelle, for a much needed drink. By the end of the evening, Freddie and the chief clerk had been anxious to catch the last train back to Southend, and a cab had been called. By the time that they had consumed a couple more and entered the cab, FG was in a bad way, and when they arrived at Fenchurch Street station, he was out to the world. At this station there is a rather long staircase leading from the road to the platforms, but in those days there were no escalators nor was there a passenger lift, and FG was a heavy six-footer. By no means could they get FG to the train, and so Joe, unbeknown to Freddie Croasdell, paid the cabbie some twenty pounds, a small fortune then, to take FG to Thorpe Bay, a journey of some forty miles and after midnight. Whilst Joe went to relieve himself, Freddie, being the gentleman, asked the cabbie what the fare would be, and without advising Freddie that Joe had already paid him, the cabbie took another twenty pounds from him and then drove off quickly. By the time the cab reached Thorpe Bay, FG was coming out of his heavy sleep. With a very bad head, he asked the cabbie how much he owed him. "Twenty pounds, guv!" came the reply, and FG paid him and stumbled indoors.

Joe had the mistaken belief that he could pave the way for those whom he had kept out until the early hours by telephoning their wives and charming the ladies into accepting the situation. It seems that, from all the feedback that I have received, far from placating the wives, his calls merely incensed them and the poor chaps would be in really deep trouble by the time they arrived home.

Just as Joe could be terse to his staff, as I had found out when I had tried to contact him before I had arrived at the branch, so he could be equally short to many of his customers. What is surprising is that although his manner usually caused an unholy row at the time, the customers usually acquiesced, and a few days later all would be sweetness and light between them again. I can vouch for the following story, because I was a witness to the whole event.

Each morning Joe and I, and perhaps the chief clerk, would have coffee at Joe's desk as we went through the morning post. We referred to these meetings as "prayers". It was Joe's practice to scan through all the cheques in the clearing in order to see where all the money was going. In truth this was good banking especially in a branch like Stepney. Apparently, on one occasion, he had sent back some cheques on a customer's account despite the fact that there was a sufficient credit balance on the account to meet them. This was something unheard of, and seemingly an outrageous action, and so the customer had thought, and he had expressed this opinion forthrightly. I happened to be in Joe's office when the distraught customer had telephoned. Joe's telephone was a deskset which could be used either through the handset, or by just speaking into it, in which case the caller could be heard quite plainly by anyone who happened to be in the room. Our blind telephonist introduced the caller and put him through. It was one of our non-*frum* Jewish traders.

"Is that you, Joe?" came the voice.

"It is," Joe replied sternly.

"What do you mean by sending my cheques back, Joe? There was plenty of cash on the account! You have no right! I shall have to see my solicitor. You have gone too far this time, Mr Holmes!" said the caller, switching from first name terms to emphasise his anger.

"You have no right to expect me to pay your gambling cheques!" Joe replied.

"There is no law against issuing cheques to my sporting club if I want to. You had no right whatsoever to return them, when there was money on the account! You get right on to the club and call the cheques back, or you are in trouble! Big trouble!"

"I shall do no such thing. You came to me only last week and arranged an overdraft for your business. When your business cheques are presented, I do not want to have to return *them* because all the facility has been used to pay your gambling cheques!" reiterated Joe, and to my amazement he put the phone down on the customer.

The telephonist kept calling to say that the customer wanted to speak to Joe, all through the day, but Joe refused to speak to him.

As we sat at "prayers" for the next two or three days, the poor telephonist, who was stuck in the middle of this feud, would ring through to say that the customer was on the phone asking to talk to Joe urgently. Joe would reply that he did not wish to talk to the customer. On the third morning of these encounters, the pleading tone of the telephonist's voice possibly had an effect on Joe, and the customer was put through.

"Hello, Joe?" came the voice.

"What do you want?" Joe asked rather brusquely.

"Well Joe, it's my boy, Izzie. He has fallen in with a bad lot, and I am worried about him."

"So what do you want me to do about it?" asked Joe curtly.

"I think you should give him one of your talkings-to."

"What talkings-to?" enquired Joe.

"You know, Joe, like you give me!"

Joe had won again, and that customer had known that Joe had been right to return those gambling cheques, however unethical and probably illegal the action might have been at the time. The lesson had been taught, and it had been learned.

Chapter Fourteen

Joe and the Festive Spirit

In the last chapter I described Directors' Inspections, whereby a team made up of local directors from outside districts would visit other designated districts and look at advances and talk to staff. Occasionally, a board director would "inspect" a district and as part of this event, one or two local directors would sweep this gentleman around by car on a flying visit to the major branches.

They would be on a tight schedule with all the branches forewarned and given a copy of the timetable. The visit usually ended with senior managers and other senior appointments within the district meeting for lunch in the local directors' dining room. For good reasons the local directors were always cagey about bringing such personages to Stepney. On the only occasion that this happened during my time at Stepney, the visiting board director was a very elderly gentleman by the name of Gurney. The name of Gurney, of course, was synonymous with banking in the Norfolk area, where the main bank had been Gurney & Co before it had been absorbed into the Barclays Group.

Mr Gurney was a very pleasant, elderly gentleman who must have been in his eighties at the time. It appeared that he had found the rush around the branches to have been be rather too much at his age. Having seen around our branch and having chatted to a couple of the staff, Mr Gurney was taken to Joe's room for the customary few words with the branch manager. I could see that the two accompanying local directors were anxiously looking at their watches because progress around the branches had been slower than they had wished. It was about eleven-thirty a.m. when Mr Gurney sat down for his chat with Joe, and it was evident that on their schedule the local directors had planned to have reached the next branch by that time, but they could not hustle poor Mr Gurney too much.

"Good morning, Mr Holmes," said Mr Gurney, smiling in a friendly fashion. I do not know if they had ever met before, or if the old gentleman had heard of Joe's reputation, but his greeting was full of warmth.

"Good morning, sir," replied Joe as he helped Mr Gurney into a comfortable chair. "Well, sir, the sun is over the yard-arm. Would you care for a nip of something to keep out the cold?" asked Joe with a friendly glint in his eye.

"Why, what an excellent idea!" came the eager response. The local directors nearly had apoplexy! "But, sir, I really do not think..." stammered one as he tried in vain to draw the old gentleman's thoughts back to the timetable.

"We'll make it a quick one then," replied Mr Gurney. The drinks were poured and very soon he and Joe had discovered a topic to chat about which was far more interesting than banking, it was horse-racing. The local directors gave up in despair.

It was at least half an hour later before the very fraught local directors eventually managed to bundle Mr Gurney into the car and to move on. The only comfort they could feel was the relief that Joe would not be in the local head office lunch party, which was attended only by senior managers whose branches had not received a visit from the board director.

Every Christmas, Stepney branch put on a party that was the envy of the East End. Anybody from Local Head Office, who was anybody, wanted to be there, except for the local directors, who as individuals would have liked to come, but, as a group, felt that they might have witnessed events that it would be better for them not to know about. Many customers came, but not the *frum*, because they could not eat non-Kosher food, and they did not drink beer or wine.

Before I describe the Christmas parties, I should perhaps describe the scenes in the branch leading up to Christmas. I have told about the amount of spirits I had found in the strong-room upon my arrival in the October. These had been just the remnants of gifts received on the previous Christmas, and some perhaps from even earlier Christmases. The reader will therefore have some understanding of the quantities of drink that was received by the branch, mainly from its Jewish customers, and in particular from the orthodox Jewish customers at Christmas time. Most of this drink was whisky, followed by gin, brandy and champagne, and then some lesser-known drinks such as Slivovitz (plum brandy) and others; they would all be for Joe. I, too, received gifts, but whereas Joe's would arrive in crates, mine would be in single bottles, for which I was none the less grateful. Many a manager even of a large branch would have been pleased to have received my share. On the days immediately before Christmas there would be queues of these bearded orthodox gentlemen sitting in the banking hall. They would be holding their gifts, each trying to hide his from the prying eyes of the others, but at the same time trying, himself, to assess his present against those that the others were bringing for Joe. Status was at stake.

Joe would greet each cordially, pretending that he did not know why the customer had come, and then his visitor would unburden himself of the bottle or crate, which he was carrying. After a few minutes a cheery farewell would be taken, and the next on the list would enter the great man's room.

The more senior of the customers would have assistants to accompany them, and they would arrive by appointment with several crates for Joe and with gifts for me and for the chief clerk, the first cashier and probably for Don Cottle. Mr FW, who kept the accounts of only a small part of his huge property empire with Stepney, would arrive by appointment accompanied by his entourage in two Rolls Royces. He would be in the first car, and would be ushered into Joe's room, to be followed by what appeared to be a safari procession of his menials bearing boxes and crates. Many were for Joe, but others were for the local directors, and for senior Local Head Office staff, since it was not thought politic for such gifts to be delivered to Local Head Office. On occasions, the local directors would often be waiting in Joe's room, in order to greet and to thank Mr FW. As soon as the gifts had been handed over, Mr FW and his lackeys would depart, leaving the local directors to party on with Joe, and with Joe Murat, who would have come down earlier from the Gallipoli with hampers of succulent sandwiches and other goodies to be washed down with champagne. The branch staff would eagerly consume the remnants of these feasts, once the local directors had left. As well as for Joe and the local directors, Mr FW's boxes would have contained gifts for myself and for most of the branch staff. By the end of the week before Christmas it was almost impossible to get into Joe's room for crates and baskets and bottles.

It was in this scenario that I witnessed a most touching scene. One of our *frum* customers was in business as a button-maker at a time when buttons were out of fashion. He had a small overdraft facility of about five hundred pounds which was guaranteed by Mr B yet was not really sufficient. Many of his cheques had been returned unpaid through lack of funds on his account during the year, and particularly in the months running up to Christmas. This poor little grey-bearded gentleman went into Joe's room amongst all the abundance of the gifts which filled the floor space. Embarrassed, he held out a half-bottle of Scotch to Joe, "Please accept my humble gift, Mr Holmes, I am sorry that it is not more," he said, eyeing all the crates piled on the floor around him. I could see that Joe was himself highly embarrassed, an emotion of which I would not have considered him capable until that moment.

"Mr R," Joe's words stumbled out, "I cannot take your kind gift."

"Please, Mr Holmes!" the other pleaded. I think that he would have gone on to say that, compared to all the gifts from other people, his gift was too humble, but that was all that he could afford; instead, he just lowered his eyes in humility.

"Mr R, I cannot take it!" said Joe almost pleading for the little man to take it back. "I have been returning all your cheques for the past two months!"

"I know," replied Mr R humbly, "but this is for all the cheques that you did not return!" and there was no suggestion of humour in his weak voice.

Joe shook his hand and thanked him profusely. After Mr R had left, Joe turned to me, for I had been in the room all the time during the interview, "What else could I do but to accept it?" he asked, and I thought that I just might have heard a frog in his throat.

I would like to put out of the reader's mind any idea that there was any form of corruption in the giving and receiving of these presents. It is true, as I indicated earlier, that some of the wealthier members of the orthodox community felt that they gained status in the eyes of their fellows by the size of the gifts that they were seen to give, but the members of the community were very generously disposed. I think that their gesture in making these gifts was one of genuine affection for their bank, its manager and its staff. Never was a cheque paid that should have been returned, never was an overdraft or a loan facility requested or granted as a result of this generosity, and I can testify to that. I would like to add that not all the presents were retained by the management and senior staff to whom they were sent, but most of the recipients would hand over some of their gifts to a general pool for all the staff to share. One of my favourite presents was the regular gift of a whole smoked salmon from our West End customers Messrs Foreman and Sons, who were acknowledged fish specialists and suppliers to the main London Hotels.

Reverting to the office Christmas party, this was, as I have already stated, a date for the diary of staff and customers alike. There was certainly no need for the branch to buy drink! Members of the women staff were given time off during the day to prepare the food. Joyce, my wife, came to help during my second Christmas at the branch, for it was a mammoth task. At Christmas 1968, my final Christmas at the branch, my daughter Pat, who was then fourteen and fond of cooking, came along with Joyce to add another pair of hands. Both Joyce and Pat very much enjoyed this chore, and although it was a hard day's work they loved working in the very friendly atmosphere created by the attitude of the staff. Later, whilst taking her A-levels, and long after I had left the branch, Pat went back to work there as a student during the summer holiday period before she went to train as a radiographer. The bank often recruited student staff in the busy summer months when there could be staff shortages. Often the more capable students would be given a till to run.

The party would begin at around six p.m., after the day's work was finished and all the cash reserve had been put away, and after the strong-room had been closed. Joe would probably have been out to lunch with some of his customer friends, and would have returned with them to enjoy a bottle in his room.

Before the party started, Solly Gritzman, who was much better known as Tubby Isaacs, would arrive from his renowned shellfish stall in Middlesex Street, more popularly known as Petticoat Lane. He would bring cartons of whelks, mussels, winkles, cockles and jellied-eels and set them out upon the counter. These were his generous gift towards the party and they were very much enjoyed by the guests.

Taxi-loads of guests would begin to arrive, and, usually, there were some very well-known people amongst them. I was introduced to the estranged wife of the top-ranked film comedian, Norman Wisdom, and to many others who were in show business at the time, and quite well-known. Joe would have all the important guests in his room, and most of the others would be in the banking hall, and some would even have climbed the stairs to find some space in the empty rooms above. The drink would be set out on the counter and Don Cottle together with Bill Webb, the first cashier, would be the main barmen. Other branch staff would attend to the refills to help them out. For security reasons we needed special dispensation from the police at Arbour Square police station to continue past nine p.m. It would be at about that time that those who had arrived first were becoming the worse for wear, and taxis would be summoned. I think that the word would get to the taxi drivers that the party was on and that Joe would not waylay them. Therefore, we would have a continuous queue of taxis outside as the partygoers started to wend their ways home at about nine-thirty p.m. Some were in quite a bad way, and one year one large young man, a clerk from Local Head Office had to be carried struggling and kicking to his cab by about five of his colleagues.

If possible, the party would be held on the last Friday before Christmas so that the branch could be cleaned up by the cleaner with assistance from the Saturday morning staff, in time for the next working day after Christmas. Some of the staff were given Saturday morning leave as certain jobs were allowed to be held over until the following Monday morning. Some of them would be paid to come in on the Saturday just to help clear up. When the party was over Joe would take about half his gifts home in a taxi laden to the gunwales. The rest of the booty would be stored in the strong-room, to be withdrawn as and when needed during the coming year.

However, there was an established ritual for the morning following the party. Joe would arrive at nine a.m., and it was the duty of the assistant manager to organise the staff to greet him with a carol as he entered the branch. He very much enjoyed the thought that the staff loved him. Actually, in holding this belief, I think that he was rather more mistaken than he would have cared to know!

Joe and I did not always get on well together, but we had a reasonable relationship in the office. On occasions he would be in one of his bad moods and, tiring of his petulance, for which I could see no good reason, I would leave the morning "prayers" and return to my room. I would give the dividing door an extra pull behind me as I went, causing it to shut with a bang, just to show my annoyance. I would then bury myself in my work for the rest of the day, making a point of avoiding Joe, not because I was sulking, but because I would feel that I did not want to speak to him unless it was really necessary. I did not wish to be rebuffed again if his mood was going continue as it had started. To the best of my recollection, his moodiest days were those when he had no plans to go out at lunch-time. As a

158

consequence he would stay in his office for most of the day. At about five p.m. I would be at my desk, attending to the usual end-of-the-day jobs of signing the post and perhaps reading the day's diary or the day's information sheets' notes. Suddenly, I would be conscious of a hand reaching over my shoulder from behind me and a tumbler of whisky would be placed in front of me. It was a peace offering. "Come along, Denis," Joe would say, "bring your drink into my room," and we would be friends again.

There was a system, unique to the London districts which had the services of gentlemen known as the Metropolitan Managers. I never really understood where they fitted into the system. Each district had its own local directors, and with assistant general managers and general managers close at hand in Head Office, I could not see the purpose of this extra tier of management. They all had been former managers of large London branches, and the only job, which I knew them to do, was to undertake property valuations for freeholds or leases whose value was in excess of one hundred thousand pounds. All property valuations were for properties that had been offered as security for bank lending. In the country districts such valuations would be carried out by managers of branches in the locality of the property to be charged to the bank, up to the amount of their lending discretions. If a property were for a higher figure, then two managers had to be involved.

Local head offices often called for professional valuations for properties of very high value, or for those with complicated leases or titles. However, in London we had these metropolitan managers who would accompany a branch manager to inspect sites of high value. Joe loved these occasions because one of these metropolitan managers was an old drinking partner. On one particular occasion this gentleman and Joe set off to carry out a valuation of the local showroom of the main Ford dealer in the Commercial Road, and a building which I daily walked past on my way from Stepney station to the office. This particular valuation took them the whole day, including lunch in the Gallipoli, and I doubt if they had parted company before midnight. A few days later an official letter was received from the Metropolitan Managers' Office, confirming the valuation. The irony was that they both knew what value they had intended placing upon the property before they had started out.

Another of our non-Jewish customers was a Surgeon Commander P Frank T, RN, a naval doctor. He was a most congenial chap, who loved to visit Joe and Freddie Croasdell when he was on leave, and often the three of them would go off on a jaunt together. Sometimes Frank would join us in the Exmouth Arms at lunch-time and play dominoes. On one occasion, his ship, the aircraft carrier HMS *Hermes*, was in Portsmouth, and Frank had invited Joe and Freddie to the ship, as his guests, for drinks in the wardroom, prior to a meal in a restaurant ashore. This gesture was in return for all their hospitality to him in London. Joe and Freddie travelled together from Waterloo to Portsmouth Harbour station, a journey that I knew well from my days in the Royal Navy.

Frank met them at the Portsmouth Harbour station, and he escorted them into and through the dockyard to his ship. As Joe and Freddie mounted the gangway and were met by the boatswain's party and the Officer-of-the-Day, they were accompanied by their Surgeon Commander host, and so were piped on board. Frank then took them into the wardroom. Freddie, who had served in the Royal Navy during the war, was determined that Joe was not going to get a chance to embarrass either Frank or himself in front of the ship's officers. Joe, as we know, lived by his own rules which he invented as he went along, and, consequently, Freddie had spelled out to Joe just how he should behave before they had arrived in Portsmouth.

Eventually, Frank indicated that it was time for them to leave, probably in order to get them out of the wardroom before Joe began to forget Freddie's instructions, as they had consumed a great deal of liquor. Up until then all had gone reasonably smoothly; however, there was embarrassment ahead of them as they left the ship. At the gangway, it appears that Joe had tried to tip the Officer-of-the-Day, telling him to give the boatswains a party, "One each apiece all round!"

As Frank in his immense embarrassment hustled them off the ship, Joe let go of the banknote that he was offering, and it fluttered around in the strong breeze before landing back on the gangway behind them, but nobody thought of stopping to pick it up!

Freddie told me that he had suggested that they should dine in an unlicensed restaurant, as he did not want any more to drink with his meal. After the meal Joe had insisted that they should go to a pub and eventually they had only just managed to catch the last train from Portsmouth to Waterloo, from where Freddie took a cab all the way to his house in Leigh-on Sea. It was three a.m. by the time he had got there, and Doris, his wife, had locked up the house for the night. Knowing that Freddie was with Joe, she had thought that they had probably stayed for the night in Portsmouth. Contrary to Joe's belief, Doris did not hold him in high regard, and she did not welcome his telephone calls trying to placate her on those occasions when Freddie was out late with him. Freddie cannot remember what happened to Joe that night. The last train to Ashtead had long since departed when they had arrived at Waterloo. When Freddie had bid Joe goodnight, Joe was talking about going for a drink! It would have been just like him to have gone to knock-up poor Ali Murat at the Windmill, Bermondsey, and it would not have been for the first time, nor the last.

I do not think that Surgeon Commander Frank abandoned his friendship with Joe after that episode, but he would have earned my sympathy if he had. He certainly did not invite Joe to any ship as his guest thereafter!

Before the banks themselves entered fully into offering insurance as a service to their customers, and as a profit earner for themselves, the branch managers were allowed to accept commissions from reputable insurance companies for introducing business from customers. The commission had to be placed to a suspense account and at the end of each quarter it would be divided into two equal parts. Half would be apportioned to the branch profits, and the other half would be apportioned to the branch manager's personal account. The amount of commission earned varied from branch to branch, depending upon the area and upon the aggressiveness of the branch manager in persuading his customers to take out insurance. Most managers could not be accused of favouring one insurance company over another, because they would run separate suspense accounts for several companies.

In many cases, however, a branch manager might have risked accusations of having made the granting of a lending facility conditional upon the borrower taking out life assurance or building and contents insurance through his agency. This condition would have been implied rather than stated outright, in so many words. Bank managers were well paid in relation to their staff and in comparison to other semi-professional people, but only the salaries of the really senior managers could have been considered to be high. To the managers of smaller branches these commissions were a welcome bonus, but they were not pensionable. In some cases, especially in large towns and in the cities, some managers' insurance commissions well exceeded their bank pay, and many were reluctant to move on from a branch that enjoyed these high insurance earnings, even for promotion. I have already mentioned how the grouping of accounts had been introduced in order to prevent branch managers from abusing their personal discretions by lending to separate limited companies controlled by the same individual. Well, when these lendings were made, especially for the purchasing of property, it was the unwritten but well-established law that all the insurances in respect of each property would be through the branch manager's agency.

It was the same with lendings to customers who borrowed for other business needs. All insurances covering the property, the stock, loss of profits etc., as well as the life assurance of the proprietors, went through the branch manager's agency as a matter of course. The insurance commissions in the East End of London must have been amongst the highest in the country. Consequently the representatives of the larger insurance companies, often ex-regular officers who had retired from the armed services, courted the managers of these branches. One, from the Royal Exchange Insurance Company, was a particular friend and drinking companion of Joe's. This was before the days

162

of the merger of the Royal Exchange Insurance with the Guardian Insurance Company. Stepney branch had built up a large folio of business with the Royal Exchange Insurance.

The majority of the highest premiums taken were from our orthodox Jewish property companies and from the businesses of our Jewish traders and from the rag trade. After the Six-Day-War between Israel and its neighbours in June 1967, there was a recession and many businesses suffered and were holding unsaleable stock. At about this time it seems that many of our customers started having fires in their warehouses, and the insurers were hard hit. Because of their representative's close affiliation with Joe, policies covered by the Royal Exchange were particularly subjected to large claims. Eventually the Royal Exchange representative pleaded with Joe not to pass any more business his way! One of our customers had made three claims for large amounts in as many months. In the 1970s the bank ended this system and opened up its own insurance departments. In compensation, the bank paid each manager a single sum for his loss of anticipated future earnings at the time.

The jewel in Joe's crown was Don Cottle. Joe knew that he could rely upon Don in any job given to him as he was meticulous in his work, and seldom made a mistake. He also responded well to the customers, but kept them well in hand, and would not allow any of the more wily ones to take liberties.

Up until my retirement in 1989, the branches had to send to Head Office, via their local head offices, what was known as the Audit Return, every autumn. These returns were passed to the external auditors of bank's own annual accounts, and were a summary of all advances and limits granted, but only the really large advances needed to be shown individually. Each year, for sampling reasons, certain districts were selected at random to show accounts of lower lending limits. The job had a nuisance value to all branches and to the local head office staff who had to vet the returns before passing them to Head Office. A dim view was taken of any branch that made mistakes or was untidy in the presentation of its audit return. Some branches had no individual lendings large enough to qualify, and needed only to complete the totals columns at the foot of the final page, whilst most other branches had only one or two accounts to report. These returns were on large white paper sheets folded to the size of a broadsheet newspaper, and had to be typed most carefully. Because of the grouping system, Stepney branch, with its four major groups (and since each individual company account within the group had to be entered), had an enormous return to compile, running into about thirty to forty pages. The typists just could not cope and so the job was given to Don Cottle, who completed it in his immaculate copperplate handwriting in pen and ink, *not in biro!* I have always admired craftsmen who can create works of art be they in pottery, furniture, jewellery or the like, and in my opinion, Don was such a craftsman. When Don had prepared and written them, Stepney's Audit Returns were truly works of art. Each year Local Head Office would bet Joe that they would find three mistakes, however trivial and, if they did, Stepney had to stand drinks and cakes for the local directors and their checking staff. If they could not find three mistakes then the local directors would have to be the hosts. Consequently, local head office would set their best clerks to scrutinise the Stepney Audit Return with painstaking care, but they never won the bet. True to their obligation, the local directors would arrive with a hamper and bottles on an evening towards the end of September every year. The toast was "Don Cottle!" In his droll way, Don was very proud of this recognition of his ability and of his worth.

Chapter Fifteen

Joe Murat and The Gallipoli:
The Retirement of Joe Holmes
Farewell to Stepney for me

Joe Murat was a Turkish Cypriot who had come to Britain before the Second World War, with his family, which had included aunts and uncles and cousins, as well as his own parents and brothers and sisters. Having started up in the usual humble ways of immigrants, beginning with a small street café, Joe had increased his empire to include a Country Club in Surrey, the L'hirondelle nightclub near to St James' Park and the Windmill drinking club in Bermondsey. Finally, he achieved his greatest ambition and created the Gallipoli Turkish restaurant in an underground building that had previously been a Turkish bath situated between Old Broad Street and St Botolph's Churchyard, not far from Liverpool Street Station. It was entirely below ground level and had no access to natural daylight.

The transformation had been very costly because of the normal problems inherent in underground buildings with regards to dampness and condensation. These problems had caused special difficulty where the kitchens had to be installed, and where hygiene regulations had to be met. In addition to this, Joe Murat had wanted to establish a Turkish authenticity about the place and, to achieve this, he had acquired a Turkish ornamental fireplace from a sultan's palace in Turkey. This was no ordinary fireplace, but was huge, and Joe Murat had it shipped to London from Turkey using the same method as the Americans had used when they had purchased the old London Bridge and had it rebuilt in the USA. With the Turkish fireplace, as it was dismantled in Turkey, every tile was individually numbered and, on arrival in London, it had been very carefully restored in the Gallipoli restaurant. In addition a special glass table had been installed to allow the belly-dancers to perform above floor level. This table would be used for diners, until the cabaret began. After the belly-dancers had performed, the table could be lowered into the floor to allow dancing for the diners. On top of all this expensive construction, which was being largely financed by Stepney branch, were the lavish furnishings acquired from the famous L— Stores. The cost of these furnishings was many thousands of pounds, which seemed extremely extravagant in 1966. L—'s was a store which had never before entered into credit arrangements, but unfortunately for the director who had authorised the Gallipoli furnishings, upon asking Joe Murat for the cash in full payment, he had discovered that the cash was not available. Consequently, L—'s were forced to give credit terms, contrary to the company's policy. L— Stores fully recouped their money as the restaurant was a great success.

The opening of the Gallipoli had taken place just a week or so before my arrival at Stepney. It had been a grand affair with the Lord Mayor of London performing the ceremony in the presence of many other dignitaries and socialites. That party had also added considerably to the overall costs, but the Gallipoli flourished for many years. Like many another debt at that time, repayment had probably been possible because of the escalating rate of inflation, which in time had diminished debts in proportion to their original liabilities. Many a bank manager had to thank inflation for helping in the recovery of bad or risky lending over the years. Any housebuyer who had bought a property for around, say, four thousand five hundred pounds in the 1960s probably found the mortgage repayments to be crippling.

After a few years though, these repayments appeared to be negligible following salary or wages increases that had come about because of inflation, together with the rise of property prices.

Joe Murat had put the running of the Windmill into the hands of his cousin, Ali. Other members of the family were employed in many manners of ways in the running of his empire. One of his chief assets was the head waiter of the Gallipoli, also named Ali, and also related to Joe Murat. Ali had a remarkable memory for the names of the clientele of the restaurant. Nothing raises a diner's self esteem more than to be recognised by the headwaiter and to receive the latter's personal attention as he enters a restaurant, especially in the company of ladies. He revels in his sense of importance when the headwaiter greets him personally.

"Good afternoon, Mr Smith, would you like your usual table?" Ali would greet the diner, even if Mr Smith had been to the Gallipoli no more than once, a year or so before! I recall a similar experience, personally, when some twenty years after leaving Stepney, I had cause to take a customer to lunch in London. It happened that the Gallipoli was close to the venue of our meeting. I had not made a booking, but, as I had walked through the door, I had heard a voice greet me. "Good afternoon, Mr Sherringham. How lovely to see you again! Would you like to be seated at your *usual* table?"!

One of the specialities of the Gallipoli was the Turkish delight which was flown into London Heathrow daily on the early scheduled airline flight, and which was collected by car to be brought direct to the restaurant. It was a very special treat for the diners.

Sadly, I understand that the Gallipoli is no longer a restaurant, and I think that its trade must have collapsed during the very bad recession of the early 1990s. Whether or not Joe Murat, Ali and the others are still living, I do not know. I hope they are, and are prospering.

The National Union of Bank Employees and the Staff Association were opposed to the bank's policy of allowing appointed staff to stay on in their positions after their usual retirement age. The bank found this extension of service to be a simple solution to its recruitment problem, but the staff representatives had pointed out that in the long term it would only serve to exacerbate the problem. Besides blocking the promotion opportunities for the rising generation of bank staff, the policy had allowed the banks to keep down the salaries of all staff including those of the appointed staff, as they had not needed to compete in the labour market for management-grade recruits from the school-leavers. This had been a short-sighted policy, which the staff representatives had considered sure to rebound on the banks when all the retained managers were eventually forced to retire, or had elected to do so. Then there would be a dearth of capable and trained staff ready to step into their shoes. The representatives had also pointed out certain dangers to the appointed staff, mainly that, if they were to die during the extended term, their widows could be at a great disadvantage financially. Instead of receiving half of the deceased's annual pension, they would have received a lump sum amounting to just one year's salary, with no pension. What was more, a manager who had extended his service would not have had the opportunity to commute a large sum from his pension for investment to provide additional income.

On an October morning in 1968, a few months before I left Stepney, Doug Hills, who was then the chief clerk, and I were at morning prayers when Joe suddenly let out a hoot of delight. He passed to us a letter from the local directors informing him that staff department at Head Office had agreed that he could stay on for a period of two years beyond his forthcoming retirement date in the spring of 1969. This, of course, called for celebration! Champagne was sent for from the strong-room, but as it was so late in the year, the branch had only a few bottles of "Israel's Finest and Most Expensive!" (according to the labels) left in the strong-room. Drinking champagne, even of the truly finest French variety, at 9.45 on a miserably wet October morning, is not to be recommended. Within a few minutes of having downed a couple of glasses under protest, I had the feeling that some workman was drilling through my head with a pneumatic drill. This sensation was to last for the rest of the day, and

Doug Hills had confided to me that he had felt exactly the same way. As for Joe, it was not a day for work – it was a day for celebration – and off he had gone, not to return until the next day.

Under a directive from the Inland Revenue, it seemed that, in order to confirm the fact that a member of staff had actually retired before continuing to serve beyond his normal retirement date, his service had actually to be broken. The employee had then to be retaken on to the staff, but I do not pretend that I fully understood this ruling by the Inland Revenue at the time, any more than I really understand their thinking upon most matters today.

As I have indicated, Joe was about six months away from his true retirement date when he received his good news, and the episode that I am about to relate certainly happened after I had returned to Chelmsford district in April 1969. It was reported to me well after the event and when I had met up with one of my old colleagues from Stepney, later. I am sure there was an element of truth in it.

Joe had reluctantly been forced to absent himself from his branch for two full days in compliance with the Inland Revenue's edict. On the first morning of this enforced absence from Stepney branch, he had awakened in his bed at home at about the usual time. Instead of having to get up, wash, shave, and have breakfast before leaving for the station to catch his train to work, it had suddenly dawned upon him that, for two days, he had retired!

"How," he had asked himself, "do the retired spend their day? Well, for a start, they have a lie in for an hour or two, until it is time to go to the pub at opening time!" So he had turned over and gone back to sleep until about ten a.m. at which hour he got up for breakfast. At about eleven-thirty a.m. he started off down the road towards his local. On the way he found a lone workman digging a hole in the pavement only a few doors away from his house. Joe reflected. In his experience, retired gentlemen always made a point of standing to watch road-menders as they dug holes in the road, and so he stood for a few minutes watching this poor chap at work. At last the workman could stand it no more, and, being a particularly civil type, he looked up at Joe, and eyeing Joe suspiciously, he said, "Good morning, governor. It's a nice day!"

"Yes," replied Joe. "You are working very hard. I understood that British workmen just sat around drinking tea all day."

"A chance would be a fine thing!" came the reply as the workman wiped his brow with his sleeve.

Joe said no more, but returned home and a few minutes later he was to be seen pushing the tea trolley along the pavement with the best tea service and silver spoons and some digestive biscuits. He and the workman sat on the edge of the hole for their tea-break chatting away like old pals. Later Joe wheeled the trolley home, before setting off once more for the pub where he had stayed until closing time, or probably a bit longer.

That evening, his two sons, one a bank employee and the other a solicitor, had arranged a party for Dorothy and Joe at a rather posh country club near Ashtead. During the early part of the evening all had gone well. There had been plenty of drinks before the meal and excellent wines to go with it, followed by liqueurs. Dorothy, of course, took very little alcohol, but it was Joe's big night. After the meal was over and whilst coffee was being served, Joe began to think that all the other diners in this very full restaurant were far too quiet. They were not really enjoying themselves! What could he do about it? He decided to get them all singing. To the immense embarrassment of his family, especially to his solicitor son, Joe stood up and started to persuade all the other rather solemn diners to join in his favourite cockney songs. Before long he was singing "I'm Forever Blowing Bubbles" and soon he was getting some of them to join in "Knees Up, Mother Brown" and to perform all the actions. Apparently most of them enjoyed it and Joe received generous applause until at last his sons had persuaded him to stop, to many cries of "Shame!" from the other tables. The applause had continued, together with cries for an encore. Joe in response, rose from his seat and having collected his bowler hat from the hat-stand, took it around all the tables, pleading that he was a poor pensioner. The other guests threw money into his hat generously. His sons and Dorothy nearly died with shame. They tried desperately to return all the money, but the diners would not take it back. "Give it to the old chap as a retirement present, he deserves it!" was the general response. The older son had taken charge of the cash and vowed that every penny would go to a deserving charity, which later it did. After his enforced break, Joe was back in his office and carried on as if he had never been away. It was a case of business as usual.

Sometimes some chance remark will prove to be a turning point in a lifetime. In the spring of 1968, I had gone to the Chelmsford District Sports Club's annual challenge match between the branches in the Southend-on-Sea area and those in the Chelmsford area. I had been honorary secretary to the Chelmsford Sports Club, Southend Section, before I had left for Stepney, and so I wanted to meet up with some of my friends. The challenge consisted of about seven events, which included five-a-side football, tennis, table tennis, netball, darts, tug-of-war and badminton. This meant that there were sports for both sexes. It was known as the Bland Trophy in the form of a silver cup, which had been given to the district by some bank dignitary many years before. Whilst the events were taking place a bar would be open for the non-participants and for the participants alike. During the meeting I had a chat with my former boss, Ken Williams. This was before the hilarious occasion of his visit to Stepney on his way to see the general managers at Head Office for his Norwich appointment. After greeting me in his usual friendly fashion, he suddenly announced that the new senior local director at Chelmsford, Mike Bendix, wanted me to succeed Don Miller as his local head office manager, when Don moved on. In the bank it is quite common for people to "leapfrog" one another, often on several occasions on the way up the ladder, so I was not at all offended to think that I was to be offered a job which Don was already doing. I knew that Don had a first-class brain, and that he thoroughly deserved any promotion that might come his way. In fact, I was quite pleased to foresee an opportunity to return to Chelmsford district and to get out of the clutches of London.

Mike Bendix had taken over from Dirk Pelley as senior local director, when the latter had gone to Head Office. I had met Mike Bendix at Wimbledon Staff College when I had been on my Stage III Managers Course, but he would not have remembered me from that brief meeting. He had lectured us on staff management and his words had been a revelation. His attitude had been so different from all that I had heard before, and I believe that this had something to do with his having been a field officer in the army when he had led his troops on to the bloody beaches of Normandy on D-day in 1944. He believed that all staff should be shown their annual reports, and that the branch manager should consult with the member of staff involved before a report was written. He had many other enlightened ideas and, like many others on the course, I was greatly impressed by his progressive views. After his talk several of us had clustered around him, and he had chatted quite freely with us. Unlike many of his contemporaries, who tended to be rather aloof, he was entirely approachable. I remember thinking, as I listened to him, that he was the type of chap for whom I would like to work. He was then the senior local director of Ipswich district, which was a smaller district than Chelmsford, but at the time I had no thoughts that he would be taking the place of Mr Pelley.

At the Bland Trophy meeting, before the evening was over, I had the chance to have a word with Mike Bendix, who confirmed his intention to offer me the job of local head office manager. The matter could not be taken farther at that time, unless something should happen within the year to alter the plans of either or both of us, and for that reason he asked me to keep our conversation to myself. I put Joe in the picture, of course, but otherwise I told no one. However, the idea had kept bugging me. At the time I had two teenage daughters and I seemed to have very little time to spend with them. I was playing rugby for the school Old Boys' side nearly every Saturday in the winter, and most of our away games were miles from the borough of Southend-on-Sea. On Saturdays, when we were playing teams in or near to London, I would take my playing kit with me and find my way to the ground by public transport, and rely upon a lift home after the game. I was just longing to move to a branch nearer to home.

At last, around February 1969, I was called to London Eastern Local Head Office, and the summons had all the signs of being in respect of a move, preferably up the ladder. This time, however, I knew before I saw the local directors what I was going to be offered. I arrived at local Head Office to see Mr (Mickey) Bolland, one of the three local directors. Although quite an affable chap, he was quite formal in the interview.

"You are probably wondering why I have called you here today," he began. "Well, we are going to offer you the position of Assistant District Manager of this district."

I was taken aback.

He seemed surprised that I did not immediately show my gratitude. I should point out that the title of assistant district manager was an anomaly because very few districts had district managers. They were not entirely extinct but the title was rather an archaic one. Most of them had been made local directors, but the title of assistant local director applied only to young men mainly from the aristocratic families who had founded the original banking houses which had amalgamated to form the end product, Barclays Bank Limited. These young fellows were really local directors under training, but the same could not be said for the assistant district managers, although many also ended up as local directors or progressed even beyond. In the bank there were two streams that were destined for the top echelons.

There were the "blue-bloods", rather like members of the House of Lords who got there through family connections, or there were the grammar school boys who got there on sheer ability. In saying this it must not be thought that all the "bloods" (as they were commonly called), were not worthy of their positions. Many were very astute, and many had been to university, but in those days, before the advent of business studies, they would have read various academic subjects. The bank had very few other graduate entries in those days, but that was all about to change, and a well-connected friend of mine was appointed to a position in Head Office Staff Department with responsibility directly under the General Manager Staff, to direct graduate recruitment into the bank. In those days it was commonly said that the City of London had been built on the backs of the grammar school boys.

To revert to my interview: "But, Mr Bolland," I uttered, "I came here in the belief that I was to be offered the job of local head office manager at Chelmsford. Mr Bendix told me that he was going to offer that job to me, about a year ago." It was Mickey Bolland's turn to look baffled. He was a stockily built man of a not unfriendly nature, and although only in his mid-forties he was quite bald beneath his bowler hat.

"Don't you want the job then?" he queried.

"Please do not think that I am ungrateful, but I had been expecting to return to Chelmsford district. May I think it over? Can I speak to Mr Bendix to see if he still wants me?"

"Very well, but you must let me know by the end of the week," and the interview was over.

I think that he was really astonished. Assistant managers did not turn down Assistant District Managers' jobs, since to receive the offer of such a job was the envied opportunity to put one's foot on the first step of the ladder to the top jobs.

The interview had been on a Tuesday, and I had to give my decision by the end of the week. Fortunately I was able to visit Mike Bendix on the Thursday, and he confirmed that the job at Chelmsford was mine if I wanted it, and that it would commence in April, about two months later. Neither local director, however, had discussed what salary I would receive. Discussing the salary at appointment interviews was just not done, and the salary was revealed only in the letter of appointment from the general managers. It was considered not to be the done thing to enquire about salary before receipt of that letter, and it was rumoured that such an enquiry by the appointee-elect could lose him the job.

I was really torn in my mind in deciding what to do. I knew that the job offered me by London Eastern district could be the opening of the stairway for me, but I felt that the time had come for me to choose between ambition on the one hand, and a happier home-life on the other. I decided that the quality of life for me and for my family was more important, and I gave Mr Bolland my irreversible decision. As a result, a swap was made between the districts. Terry Bradley, assistant manager at Grays branch, went to the ADM's job at London Eastern Local Head Office, and I returned to Chelmsford. I think that fate must have played its hand in some of these moves, as Grays branch had been in London Eastern district until some boundary changes had been made at an earlier time. Furthermore, I had met Terry on the Supervisors' (OC-Mech) course in 1957, when he had been machine-room supervisor at Bow, a London Eastern district branch. I am very pleased to report that this move certainly opened-up the opportunities for Terry who eventually reached the level of senior regional director in Nottingham district, in the new grouping system that was introduced by the bank shortly before we both retired.

I must confess that I had felt very cheated when upon opening my appointment letter for the Chelmsford job, I had found that my salary was to be raised by a pittance. It was to be about two thousand pounds per annum and much less than I would have received had I taken the ADM's job. Had this information been made available to me at the interview, my career might have taken a different route. I had complained, but it had done me no good, and possibly I had even muddied the waters. It seemed so absolutely unfair that it should have been considered taboo to talk about salary at a promotion interview, especially when it had been necessary for me to make a choice between the two jobs. It would have been no good me asking the holders of the jobs what their salaries were, because all staff salaries were then still linked to the seniority of the job holder, according to his age or length of service, and there were no set pay scales. Such pay scales were to be introduced a couple of years later under the new "Rate-for-the-Job" legislation. Then the branches were to be graded and managers would be appointed to branches with a known starting salary for the grade.

There are a couple more matters that I wish to comment upon before I leave Stepney. First, if anything that I have written implies that Joe Holmes did no work, then I shall have failed miserably, because Joe was a brilliant banker. He had the clever, calculating mind of a genius and could analyse any lending proposition put before him by his customers, merely by listening to it just once. He would speak his mind quite frankly to any rogue, time-waster or fool. He would help the genuine applicants who might be rather inexperienced or uncertain by either showing them how to go about improving their businesses or by pointing out the risks that they would be taking should he be foolish enough to sanction the advances which they sought. His opinions were accepted and respected by our customers and by the local directors alike. His mind was always as sharp as a razor, despite the fact that he rarely had much sleep after his escapades. He could prepare the most complicated of applications to Local Head Office or even for those which Local Head Office would need to pass up to Head Office for sanction. His reports and recommendations were always concise and to the point. Joe could do more work in the few hours that he spent at the branch than most other managers could achieve in a twelve-hour day.

If he had a fault, it was that he took no interest whatsoever in the administration of the office. He could not see why he should since he had a chief clerk who was paid to do it, and he had an assistant manager to see that the chief clerk did his job. I think that he had a point, but I also believe that a manager should show interest in his staff and in their welfare. I have hinted that Joe was not loved in the branch to the extent that he believed he was, and this was because many of the staff thought that he did not know that they existed. This attitude led to an attitude by some of the staff, though certainly not by all, that if the manager did not care about the way the office was run, why should they? I believe very firmly in the old maxim, "If there is trouble at the bottom, first look at the top."

The second point that I want to make is that Joe had a wonderful secretary. Kathy was no mini-skirted bimbo, but she was a homely, round-faced, jolly woman in her early forties. She lived in Hackney and had a jolly cockney manner that went with a loud laugh. Kathy was ideal for Joe because she was an excellent typist and, with her bubbly manner,

Joe could never turn upon her when in one of his moods. She always had his important work ready to sign before he went on his jaunts, and she would get me to sign his less important letters and reports on his behalf, later in the day. She ran his appointment lists and knew precisely the people Joe would see and when, and she got rid of those whom he would not wish to be bothered with by directing them to myself or to Don Cottle or to the securities staff.

Sadly, Kathy died just short of her retirement date, around 1986. At the time of her death I was manager of Basildon branch, and news had reached me by some means or other that Kathy was suffering from terminal cancer, and was spending her last days in the well-known St Joseph's Hospice in the Cambridge Road, Hackney. I telephoned Stepney branch to get all the details. I managed to contact Joe, who, of course, had retired much earlier, and we arranged a meeting at Stepney branch.

On the day I caught the train at lunch-time from Basildon to Stepney, and Joe and I went into John Holland's, as we remembered the Exmouth Arms, for a pie and half-a-pint, just like the old days. By the time of our re-union, most of the old buildings in the Commercial Road around and including the old branch at 451 had been demolished, but the Exmouth Arms had been saved by the intervention of the late John Betjeman, as I have mentioned earlier. It was even more crowded than I could remember from the former days. Joe was in one of his offhand moods, but we took the bus up the Cambridge Heath Road to the hospice where we saw poor Kathy. She was dozing most of the time as she was receiving strong sedation to relieve her pain. She looked so tiny, this poor lady who had been so round and jolly. When she awoke, briefly, she was pleased to see us. She had never married but had a good friend, another single lady, and also a secretary to the manager of another large branch. This lady had been collecting Kathy and taking her for car rides in the country until in the end this was no longer possible. Both had been due to retire about a year later and they had planned to go abroad on a holiday, something that neither of them had done before but, as Kathy squeezed my hand, she whispered, "It is sad, but it was not meant to be." She had then dozed off again, and Joe and I slipped away back into the street, I went back to my branch, and Joe went home, not to a pub or restaurant as he would have done in the old days. I was never to meet Joe again. We always exchanged Christmas cards up until his death. Freddie and I went to Joe's funeral in Ashtead, where we met up again with Dorothy and Joe's two sons, and with friends and colleagues from the past, including Jimmy Groves, my predecessor as Joe's assistant manager. By then Jimmy had taken early retirement.

One of my great regrets was that I did not go to Kathy's funeral. I had asked one of the staff, who was still at the branch from my day, to let me know when the end came. It did not seem right to keep telephoning to see if Kathy was still alive, but after about ten days, and not having heard anything more I had telephoned only to discover that Kathy had been cremated on the previous day. She had died a day or two after I had seen her for the last time, and they had forgotten to advise me.

Joe finally retired in 1971. He held his party at a licensed restaurant in Mark Lane, but, to my surprise, it was not the lavish event that I had expected. I went by train to the close-by Fenchurch Street station and to my surprise I was able to take my leave fairly early. He had plenty of his old drinking chums around him and I doubt if he realised that I had gone.

Chapter Sixteen

Life After Stepney

There is no doubt that I would have been happier working as an assistant district manager in London Eastern than being Local Head Office Manager in Chelmsford. In London Eastern Local Head Office, I would have been one of three ADMs, and I feel that I would have benefited from the comradeship of my other two colleagues, and would have learned from them. As it was I had elected to go to Chelmsford for the sake of my home life and I had no right to complain, but once again I felt that I was a misfit. Although I was there for three years almost to the day, I always felt that I was not right for the job. One of my weaknesses is the fact that I am uncomfortable in the presence of my superiors, and in Local Head Office there were three of them, and they were all local directors.

I do not wish to write more about my role in Local Head Office, except for the fact that there were many major changes that had to be coped with. These tasks included the advent of the Industrial Relations Act, the introduction of the new Rate-For-The-Job policy and the merger with Martins Bank. I was fortunate enough to have been able to persuade Mike Bendix, the senior local director to poach Jean Temple from London Eastern district. Without Jean I do not know how we would have coped with the volume of work that the provisions of the Industrial Relations Act and the implementation of Rate-For-The-Job had brought upon us. With regards to the merger with Martins Bank, we in Chelmsford were regarded as being lucky because we were unique, I think, being the only district which had no branches of Martins Bank in its area. However, ex-Martins staff were transferred into our district and this did cause problems because of the difference in the pay structure. Like Lloyds Bank who would have joined in with this merger had not the Monopolies Commission ruled against it, the staff of Martins Bank had to contribute towards their pensions from their pay, but we in Barclays did not. The whole thing was an anomaly because the staff of Martins, as did the staff of Lloyds, received higher pay than staff of Barclays to compensate them for these payments.

Outsiders always regarded it as a take-over of Martins Bank by Barclays. From the date of the merger it seemed to all the Barclays staff that the top jobs suddenly started going to the former staff of Martins. It certainly appeared to be so, if one looked at the appointments of the uppermost positions in the bank, thereafter.

Suffice to say that as Local Head Office Manager, I was given a modest discretion for sanctioning advances submitted by the managers of the smaller branches, and I was responsible for the smooth running of Local Head Office. Besides Jean Temple, who was responsible for the women staff of the district, there was a lady premises secretary who worked with the local directors in administering the premises for the whole district. The office work was under the control of a chief clerk, who had two assistants, both selected for being capable of vetting applications for large advances put up by the branches. When applications for advances were received, after checking that all the relevant material, such as balance sheets and profit and loss accounts or valuations had been enclosed, their job was to search through the files to collect any other past material that may influence the local directors in their decisions. Usually the local directors would encourage these clerks to add their comments and recommendations, since they were really the pick of the younger unappointed staff of the district and were possibly being groomed for early promotion to appointment level. There was a general typist in the office, but each local director had his personal secretary, one of whom was the young lady from Rochford who had enquired if our customer and his wife "were peeing well"!

The local directors had their own dining-room where on most days they entertained customers who had been brought along by their branch manager to discuss business and to meet the local directors. Some of the more important customers made frequent visits to Local Head Office and were well-known to the local directors. On other occasions staff, mostly senior or appointed, would be entertained at their table. Often the table would be made up of a mixture of both groups.

The dining room was run by the combined efforts of Lucy, the lady cook, and Ernest, the local head office messenger. These two were a comedy act. Lucy who was quite small and grey-haired, must have been in her late sixties, and had a reputation for hen-pecking the messenger. She had a great tendency to panic when confronted with a large luncheon or dinner party, although she always provided an enjoyable meal efficiently. Ernest, or Ernie as he was more commonly called, was a most affable and well presented chap, in his early forties. Ernie had the propensity to be a walking disaster at times, and Lucy could often be heard castigating Ernie for his latest calamity in the kitchen.

On one particular occasion the local directors had asked Lucy to arrange a buffet for about forty people, far more than the usual maximum of ten guests or less, for whom she normally had to provide a sit-down meal. Out of hearing from the local directors, she began to panic. "How can I possibly manage?" she had moaned. It happened to be during the schools' holiday period, and after checking with my wife, Joyce, I arranged for Joyce, and our two teenaged daughters to come and help her in the kitchen. That seemed to placate Lucy for a while, but when they arrived, instead of welcoming and organising them she threw her hands in the air and cried, "I prefer to be in my own kitchen by myself with the door shut!" Eventually Joyce managed to calm her down and the job was done, and was pronounced to be a huge success by the local directors. Lucy then had the grace to turn to Joyce and my daughters and say, "Thank you very much, I just do not know how I should have coped without you!"– which I thought was a handsome gesture. At home even to this day we joke about wanting "to be in our own kitchen with the door shut"!

Ernie's main job was to keep the dining room clean, which he did well, and also to act rather as a butler and to serve at table. Afterwards he would clean all the silver, and generally help Lucy, when she would let him. He was quite good at this, but he often got things wrong, such as forgetting to put out the condiments, or not putting out fish knives and forks when fish was on the menu. I usually tried to run my eye over the table each day, before the guests arrived to see if I could see any mistakes in laying-up the table. Even later, after I had moved on from Local Head Office, I could not drop the habit of running my eye over the table as I brought my guests into the dining-room. On one occasion I had to pull Ernest aside and point out that there were eight for lunch and that he had laid up for only six. This would have been embarrassing when the local directors and guests had gone to sit at table. Actually on one very embarrassing occasion as the guests had gone to the table, it was discovered that there were two places less than there were guests. This was not Ernie's fault, but, through a misunderstanding between the secretary of the local director who had responsibility for the dining room and Lucy, there had been a mistake in the numbers attending. Fortunately the first course had been soup, and this was made to go round, but the main course was of individual steaks, and the exact number had been prepared. The error was discovered far too late for the cook to send out for more, and two local directors had to pretend that they preferred corned beef. Luckily there was a choice between a sweet or cheese and biscuits and so further embarrassment was avoided.

Ernie's other job was to act as Mike Bendix' chauffeur to avoid Mike driving and drinking whenever he had to go to a social function. Ernie also had to clean Mike's car, and to take it to the garage when a service was due. On more than one occasion he had an accident driving it to or from the garage. The most memorable time was the eve of the day when Mike and Ingrid, his wife, and their teenage daughter were due to drive to the Camargue for their holidays. As usual, Ernie had taken the car in order to fill it with petrol when, on the return journey, he had been in collision with another vehicle with the inevitable result; thus the holiday had to be delayed until the car had been repaired.

The worst job that I had at Local Head Office came one morning when Mike Bendix had called me to his room. His two colleagues were out, and it was necessary for him to discipline one of the managers, who had very unwisely granted himself a loan in a fictitious name. This was because Local Head Office had declined to give him a higher bridging loan pending the sale of his house, upon appointment to his first branch as manager. Consequently, I was to be the witness to this disciplining. The manager had been transferred from the Southend area to a country branch, and it was his first managerial appointment after many years as a chief clerk. In the opinions of Local Head Office and of the manager of the branch in the area of his home, the price that he was asking for the sale of his Southend house was much too high. He would in that case face a long wait until a buyer could be found, or, if the house-market had not come out of the doldrums, he would have been forced to reduce the price. This would have left him with insufficient funds to repay the bridging loan in full from the proceeds. In those days bank staff were treated very generously for their house purchases, and staff home loans were at the very generous fixed rate of two-and- a-half per cent per annum. When managers or chief clerks were appointed to branches in areas some distance away from their previous branches, and where the house moves were made at the bank's behest, bridging loans were granted free of interest. In most cases the bank preferred the senior staff of its branches to live in the towns or villages where they worked. This did not usually apply to London or other large city centres, of course.

On the morning in question, Mike Bendix had indicated that I should sit with him behind his desk and then he had sent for the culprit. On entering, the manager had courteously acknowledged us both and then Mike had indicated to him to sit down in front of the desk. What followed took me by surprise, but it completely shattered the accused man, who, I suspect, had expected a severe reprimand or, at worst, demotion back to chief clerk. Mike Bendix was renowned for standing up for his staff through thick and thin, even getting himself into bad odour with Head Office. He would fight for the interests of members of the staff of his district.

"R," he burst out, with the first name of the man before us, "I have got to sack you!"

The man was staggered. "Oh no, Mr Bendix, not the sack!"

"I'm afraid so, there is no choice."

I felt awful because it had been on my recommendation to the relevant local director that the bridging loan should not be increased. The reasoning was correct under the circumstances, and the local director had agreed with me. R had not stolen any money, and he had intended to pay every penny back, but by raising a loan in a fictitious name he had committed fraud, and that was unforgivable. A machinist working in his branch had noticed his action and she had, as they say today, "blown the whistle" on him. From that day on Mike Bendix went out of his way to help R to purchase a small business, and authorised loans to enable him to get started.

Upon returning to the Chelmsford district, I became a member of the Thorpe Bay Yacht Club. I could not foresee our daughters taking up rugby football, and so, in an effort to keep the family together Joyce and I had purchased a Mirror dinghy. These dinghies were all the rage in the 1960s and 1970s. Barry Bucknell, who was a famous DIY show presenter on BBC television, had designed them. Mirrors could be bought in kit form, but we had bought ours second-hand from a club member.

I had joined the club in order that our daughters should receive good tuition and mix with sailing enthusiasts. No sooner had I taken this step than Bert Hattey, my former manager at 45 Victoria Avenue, had twisted my arm to take over the job of Honorary Treasurer of the club from him. Having been retired from the bank for about three years, he and his wife had decided to move to Cornwall. I was soon to learn that taking on this job was a great mistake, because it was a large club with many members and sections and there was so much work to do. There were bar stewards to hire and occasionally to fire, subscriptions to collect, and brewers to be paid among other numerous jobs. There was no opportunity to entertain thoughts of sailing in the Mirror dinghy.

I relate this fact because, in my position as Local Head Office Manager, it was one of my duties to organise all the functions in the district for the local directors, except for those organised by the local bank sports club. Barclays Bank, as a whole, had a sailing club with several fine sailing cruisers and yachts, as well as a dinghy section. Most of the larger boats were based either on the Solent at Southampton or on the Thames at Putney, or thereabouts. The sailing club was very popular with the upper echelons including the general managers, and the board directors. Every year the sailing club would organise a dinghy regatta, usually at a different venue around the country, and in 1971 they selected Thorpe Bay Yacht Club. I was now in the very difficult situation of having to wear two hats. On the one hand I had to negotiate for the bank with the Thorpe Bay Yacht Cub for the sailing club's regatta dinner which was to be held in the clubhouse. On the other hand it was my duty to get the best deal for the Thorpe Bay Yacht Club.

I had made my position clear to both parties and had suggested that somebody else should represent either the bank or the yacht club, but nobody wanted the job. Both parties had expressed their confidence in me and I was left to juggle the two balls in the air. The deputy chairman of the bank, Mr Timothy Bevan, took part in the sailing, and presided on the top table at the dinner. He made a few humorous remarks about me to amuse those present, which included members of the bank sailing club and their guests who were mostly members of the Thorpe Bay Yacht Club. Nevertheless, he was also complimentary about my efforts. All had gone well, or so it had seemed.

Whilst at Local Head Office I had begun to understand more about how the bank was managed from the top levels. Life at Local Head Office and above was mainly about internal politics. I am not saying that the local directors did not pull their weight for their districts or for the bank as a whole, and I know of none who did not. Nevertheless a great deal of time was employed by the more ambitious in scheming and manipulating in their endeavours to climb the ladder towards the boardroom. They seemed to think that it was essential to pin their flags to the mast of a rising star in Head Office, and that it was essential to identify the eventual winner of any contest in advance. If the contender that they had backed were to sink, then they would most likely sink with him, or so it had seemed to me. If I had ever harboured any thoughts of achieving local director status, then I had quickly disposed of those ambitions after witnessing all the intriguing that appeared to be the order of the day at that level. Besides, it was almost impossible for the local directors to live a life of their own. Unless they were out visiting branches or customers it was necessary for them to lunch with guests in the dining room. Often there were dinners or parties which they were expected to attend in the evenings, as well as district events. Frequently they would be expected to provide a bed at their home for visiting dignitaries from Head Office, sometimes for two or three evenings. Such a lifestyle was not for me. A branch manager's position had much more appeal to me. I hankered after being the captain of my own ship, enjoying first pick of the holiday rota, and running the branch to suit my own preferred methods.

In April 1972 I left Local Head Office to take control of my first branch, 211 Hamlet Court Road, Westcliff. It had formerly been one of the top four branches in the borough of Southend-on-Sea, and would have been considered, by most standards, a medium-sized branch for a town location. With about eighteen members of staff, it did not qualify for an assistant manager and most of its accounts were personal accounts or those of small businesses, shopkeepers and the like. I took over from the late Geoff Bryant upon his retirement. Geoff was a very much respected manager, but he came from the old school and we had little in common in our respective ideas about managing a branch. Except for some accounts belonging to the Southend General

Hospital, we had no local authority accounts worthy of mention. Among the personal accounts were many of the nursing staff of the hospital. We had the account of the Essex County Bowling Club and the account of the All England Women's Hockey Association. The bulk of our business was Jewish, and I suspect that the local directors had borne in mind my experiences with the Jewish communities at Stepney when they had appointed me to Westcliff. It seemed to me that I had not greatly benefited myself by having complied with the ideas stated by Mr Ling, the general manager, staff, in 1965. His view was that appointed staff should be prepared to switch districts in order to improve their career prospects. My colleague who had then been assistant manager at the main Chelmsford branch had been appointed manager of the prestigious branch at Chichester, following his first full managerial appointment to Rayleigh, Essex branch shortly after I had gone to Stepney. At the time of my transfer to Stepney, he had refused a similar move to a London branch.

Our Jewish customer-base at Westcliff soon made me welcome into the area. They were not as *frum* as the strict orthodox sects from Stamford Hill or Stoke Newington, but most attended the synagogue and Rabbi Shepson was much revered, and, I suspect, much feared! They soon realised that I had been groomed by the "Rabbi of Stepney", as Joe Holmes had been affectionately known. Joe had laid great store by his knowledge of the laws and practices of the strictly orthodox sect, and often questioned the rabbis among our customers until he had gained a better knowledge than many of the more liberal Jewish customers. Much of this knowledge had rubbed off on me.

Marketing was the coming thing, and I had decided to put Westcliff branch to the fore. With the co-operation of a very able staff we had really pioneered the way for about a year before most of the other branches, or even Local Head Office, for that matter, had got started.

Outside of the banking hall, the branch building was a hive of small rooms situated on two floors There was a bank flat above that, which was occupied by members of Barclays staff, but they were not employed at 211 Hamlet Court Road.

My secretary and the typists were situated on the first floor; this was not very practical. Fortunately, I was able to persuade the local directors to approve a re-build along the lines of an open-plan ground-floor office. This meant that walls had to be knocked down, and the staircase re-sited, and the whole building was a mess of dust and rubble for several months. During the re-build it was not a very pleasant place to work, besides not being conducive to increasing the business base, but once it had been finished the result was a far better branch for customers and for the staff, and was far more efficient.

We began to pick up the accounts of property developers, one of whom was developing an area in Scunthorpe. I went there to see the site for myself, before arranging the necessary finance through Local Head Office. Whilst there I met the builder whom the developers were employing on the site, David Wraith. The area under development was a former beech woodlands. David with his father, Frank Wraith, an ex-steel worker in Scunthorpe, together with their workforce of about five bricklayers and carpenters were building quality houses with double garages in this attractive parkland setting around a lake. These properties were of superior construction to many comparable properties, then being erected in haste in the Southend area, and they were on the market at less than half the price. Purchasers who were prepared to leave the south-east of England, could sell their houses for a handsome profit and move to Scunthorpe and, after paying cash for one of these delightful new houses, could invest a large sum in order to supplement their incomes.

The story is worth telling. David Wraith was about twenty-eight when I met him. He had been a site-foreman when he was only twenty-five for one of Britain's largest building companies, John Mowlem, when they had rebuilt the Addenbrookes Hospital, Cambridgeshire. One of the two directors of the development company had been the site agent, and had recognised David's ability.

The site was being developed by a number of companies, and our company was by no means the major player. David and his wife, Shirley, occupied one of the first houses built on the site. I tried always to make it a point to see such sites for myself, and to meet the people involved. It was a long way to Scunthorpe, but the reason that I had travelled there to see the site was because of the unsatisfactory reply to my enquiries about the site given by Barclays' local manager. It had read: "A reclaimed woodland area which will be axle-deep in mud in the winter months, and infested with mosquitoes from the pond in the summer"! The irony was that when I asked David if he and Shirley had been the first to move on to the site, he had replied in all innocence, "No, the bank manager, next door, in number 2, moved in a week before us." It was the same manager who had written the damning report about the site! Nevertheless, I managed to persuade the local directors to support this project for my customers, the developers, despite the local manager's damning report and, thankfully, the project was a great success.

I did not have David's accounts at that time as he then banked with Lloyds Bank in Scunthorpe. One day he telephoned me in desperation. He put forward a proposition to me that was so watertight that I could not believe that his own bank would not help him. I agreed on the spot, and within a few days David's personal and company accounts were at Westcliff-on-Sea. In those days his accounts were quite modest, but later he had seen an opportunity in the Portakabin-type relocatable-building business. He formed a company called Wraith-Rent-A-Unit and made such a success of it that he became one of my biggest, if not *the* biggest, customers, outside any of the public corporations who banked with me at my next branch at Basildon. Eventually David sold-out to the Godfrey Davis Group for several million pounds. During the time that we were doing business together, David had become chairman of Scunthorpe United FC. On one occasion he and Shirley had invited Joyce and me to a special charity match in which famous players from the earlier days had taken part. At the buffet held in the boardroom after the game Joyce and I met such famous people as Kevin Keegan and Jack Charlton. Joyce and Jack Charlton's wife had quite a long conversation. Banking opened many doors to me over the years, and I had the privilege of meeting many famous people, whom I would only otherwise have read about or seen on television or in the newspapers.

When the district marketing officers first visited 211 Hamlet Court Road, they came into my room and ask me such rudimentary questions as, "What is your patch?" They had expected me to show them a map of the area around Hamlet Court Road. "My patch," I would reply, "is here!" and I would show them a map of the British Isles. I would point out that we had obtained accounts from all over the country. These accounts, however, were not the accounts of newsagents and ladies' clothes shops and the like, but many were the accounts of the types of business that were not to be found in the borough of Southend-on-Sea. They would not be satisfied, since such answers did not fit in with the itemised questionnaires that they were required to complete.

An amusing incident happened at the branch of Midland Bank, situated almost opposite our branch in Hamlet Court Road. Norman Clark, the manager, who was a friend of mine, gave me the story which was later in the evening editions of the local *Evening Echo* newspaper. The cashier at the counter of Norman's branch was serving a youngish man. He was paying in some transaction, probably a money transfer to a hire purchase company. This transaction coincided with a representative of a local building society taking out bundles of notes from his briefcase at the next counter. This representative was paying in a large credit for transfer into his society's bank account in London. Seeing this, the young man suddenly grabbed a bundle of notes from the counter before they had been passed through to the cashier, and fled the building with them.

What he had forgotten was that his full name and address had been written upon the voucher that he was paying in at the time, and which, in his haste, he had left with the cashier who was serving him. The police were notified immediately, and the would-be bank robber found them waiting for him when he arrived home. To add to his misery, when the police called at his flat, they recognised his flatmate, who was lying on the sofa. This man was on the wanted list in connection with some burglaries that had been committed in the area. They carried out a search of the flat and recovered many stolen items. Needless to say they had also discovered other crimes for which charges could be laid against the bank snatch-thief.

It was whilst I was at Westcliff in the early 1970s, that the big break-through came in the bank salary structures, and managers' salaries leapt forward. In addition bank cars which previously had been provided for the managers of only the very top branches suddenly became available to managers of medium-sized branches. Other benefits such as private health care were added to the package. Joe Holmes had been allotted a car around 1967, when the first managers' car scheme had been introduced for the most senior managers. Like most other London branch managers, Joe did not need his car for business, and he certainly did not wish to drive to work in it. The fact was that Joe could not drive, and his new Rover car was used solely by his wife, Dorothy, who would drive Joe out in it occasionally. This was all very proper because the cars were not provided for bank business purposes, but were an undisguised perquisite to bring bank staff in line with other businesses who provided cars in their efforts to attract good managerial-grade staff.

Although excellent for the serving staff, the increase in salaries suddenly put those ex-staff, who had retired prior to the introduction of the new salary scale, to a great disadvantage. Their retirement pension had been based upon their final salary, and it was not long before their pensions began to look a pittance. Also included in the better salary scale was the index-linking of bank pensions, which did not apply to earlier pensions. Although small annual increases have been granted to the non index-linked pensions through out the years, they have not been of much comfort to the recipients because of the very low base from which they had started. Managers of medium-sized country branches, who really did need cars to get to work and to visit their customers, many of whom would be farmers situated in widespread rural areas, no longer had to run their own vehicles into the ground when out on bank business.

During my time at Westcliff there had been changes to the local directors. Those with whom I had worked had moved on or retired, but Mike Bendix had remained in charge of the district. About three years into my stay at Westcliff, I had experienced one or two acrimonious exchanges with Local Head Office, and once again, I was feeling myself to be a misfit. I explored what opportunities there were to join another bank, and, if it had been practical, I should have liked to have joined a smaller bank such as the Co-operative Bank. In such a bank, I felt that I would have had the potential to rise to a senior level, especially as some of these smaller banks were looking to venture into the small-business end of the corporate lending market. There was, of course, the problem of whether or not the bank would allow me to break the embargo placed upon bank staff not to transfer to another United Kingdom bank within a period of five years. I therefore had an interview with the United Bank of Africa, at the London Bridge branch of the Moscow Narodny Bank, where applicants for an advertised post in the UBA Lagos office were being assessed. After my interview, I was given to understand that I had a good chance of getting the job, and the salary and conditions were favourable. My problem was, however, the obvious one of having to take my wife and family with me, to a rather unstable city with a bad reputation in many respects.

One day in early 1976, after four years at Westcliff, I had been called to Local Head Office by one of the local directors to explain my attitude and although I had done nothing to deserve a reprimand, I was warned to watch my step in the future. Shortly after this contretemps, Mike Bendix had telephoned me at home, one evening. It was evident that I was still in his bad books.

"Denis," he said, "I was going to give you Basildon branch on the retirement of the present manager, but your recent attitude has made me think again!" I just listened. I did not really want Basildon, which at that time was hardly any larger than Westcliff. This switch to the New Town environment was, in my opinion, a punishment in itself. I knew that few other managers in the district would have wanted Basildon branch. I sensed that Mike was awaiting some comment from me. I told him that I was sorry if I had offended him as it had not been my intention to do so. He then confirmed that my next move was to be to Basildon. The move took place in April 1976. It was to be my last move in my career in Barclays, and in returning there as manager, the prophecy that Stuart Barker, my former manager there, had made when I had departed in 1961, had been fulfilled.

Chapter Seventeen

Basildon: The Struggle in a New Town Environment

The new branch building, into which the branch had moved in 1961 from the original gas-lighted wooden hut, had already been rebuilt to accommodate more staff. My new manager's office was in a bay suspended out from the first floor above the branch entrance. Until the rebuild, this part of the first floor had been a restaurant.

In those days the status of branches had been based upon what was known as the Branch Manager Grading system, and the initials BM prefixed each grade. The numbers ranged from the smallest branches to have a manager appointed, i.e. BM1, which would have had a total staff of about five, to the very largest branches at BM9. Each step up the ladder was rather akin to the seismic numbers for measuring earthquakes, in that moving up the scale by one point indicated almost the doubling of the size of the branch from its previous rating. Westcliff had been a BM5, but Basildon, when I joined it, was a BM6. However, the two businesses were totally different. At Westcliff our main business base had consisted mainly of small company accounts and of personal accounts. The total lendings at Westcliff, however, were far higher than those of Basildon, which at that time carried a lending book of less than half a million pounds. The credit balances were about twice that amount, but just one farming customer, who had been forced to sell land to the Basildon Development Corporation under a Compulsory Purchase Order, accounted for a sixth of that amount on just one deposit account. This balance was very vulnerable as the customer could have bought more land or invested the sum elsewhere for a higher income at any time. The reason for Basildon having a higher BM number than Westcliff was because of its large staff. The counter was particularly busy with hundreds of non-account holders using the branch to pay in their hire-purchase repayments. In addition the branch had to service the accounts of companies who had continued to bank in the areas where the businesses had originated after they had taken up factories on the new Basildon industrial estates, or offices in the newly created office blocks in the New Town. The branches where the accounts were domiciled got all the benefits of the credit or debit balances on their customers accounts whilst poor Basildon had to do all the work.

Once I had settled into Basildon, I made it my job to go after those customers to persuade them to bring their accounts to Basildon. This action did not please the managers of the account-holding branches, most of which were in London, but eventually I persuaded very many of the account holders to consider the advantages of having a manager near at hand. I told them that I was willing to go out to their factories and offices to discuss their business with them on the site, rather than for them to have to travel to see their remote manager, cap in hand. In addition to Barclays' customers, I also went around the industrial areas "cold-calling" on the customers of the other banks whose businesses were in Basildon, but who banked outside of the town. However I did not attempt to poach the accounts of the local branches of the other banks. So many of these business men were amazed that a bank manager was prepared to go to their factories to discuss their banking arrangements, and take an interest in their products. Often it was said to me by customers of both Barclays and other banks, "You know, I have banked at X branch of Barclays (or of Y bank) for thirty plus years, and the manager has never once called to see our factory." Besides the factories, we also went for the professionals, solicitors and accountants, and we were very successful. Eventually, in 1981, because we were growing so fast, we had to move the management and the securities section to new premises. We therefore took a floor in a new suite of offices close to the new Eastgate development. The branch lendings, credit balances and profits had increased many-fold. I had sensed that, having blotted my copybook with Local Head Office, my road to promotion was probably blocked for the rest of my career, and the only way that I could circumvent this embargo would be to increase the status of Basildon, thus obtaining my promotion that way. If I was the driving force leading a powerful management team in the growth of the branch, then the powers-that-be could hardly find an excuse for removing me from Basildon. The branch had advanced to a BM8 by about 1987, and it was not through my efforts alone, because I was fortunate in having a succession of very bright young men in my management team.

By 1987, Mike Bendix had retired, and Peter R, who had been one of two assistant managers at Cambridge Circus branch in my Stepney days, had become our new senior local director. In those Stepney days, the main accounts of the Freshwater Group had been at Cambridge Circus branch, and it had often been necessary for me to speak to Peter or the other assistant manager about the overall group position.

On the occasions of the annual review of my performance I, like other managers, would be called to be interviewed by Peter, who was a kindly man. Peter would interview two managers, one before lunch and the other after lunch, and both managers would join the local directors for lunch alongside the other guests for that day.

At these interviews, Peter would congratulate me on the year's results and say that they could not be bettered, but he would end up giving me a grade B+ mark. I would then pretend to be naïve and ask, "Peter, you tell me that my efforts cannot be bettered. We have put on business in all areas, and yet I cannot get my A assessment, where am I going wrong?" It was unkind of me, because I knew full well that my career was being blocked from above. Poor Peter would try to think up reasons that might satisfy me and spare his embarrassment at the same time.

Before I retired in 1989, and largely because of the policy of the grouping of branches, Basildon had taken over the neighbouring branches of Laindon and Pitsea. This had not been well received by the residents of Laindon in particular, because Laindon had been the main town and business area in that part of Essex. The creation of the new town of Basildon had not been welcomed by all. Basildon branch was upgraded to a Business Centre, and I had been promoted to business centre manager. The branch had then qualified as a BM9, the top grade, but, by that time the former local director, with whom I had a contretemps in my Westcliff days, had become a general manager. When he had heard that Basildon had qualified for BM9 rating he had declared, I was reliably informed, that Basildon would get that grading "only over my dead body!" Consequently, the upgrading was refused, but I was advised that I could appeal against the decision. Both the staff bodies wanted me to appeal, and stated that they would support me, as it was a complete injustice to withhold my promotion. However, when I looked through the schedule of salaries for a BM9 branch, I realised that I would be the only member of staff who would qualify for a rise upon the upgrading of Basildon. Secondly, the Business Centre had only just crept into the required figures, and I would not have wished to take the upgrading through an industrial dispute procedure, only for something unforeseen to happen that might cause the Business Centre to slip back on the next assessment, twelve months later. Under those circumstances my upgrading would have remained, but, had I remained at the branch, I would have been taking a salary to which I was not really entitled. I therefore told Peter R that, since I would be the only member of staff to enjoy any benefit, it was not my wish to challenge the ruling of the general manager, and Basildon remained a BM8. However on the next review in the following year, which was also my final year before retirement, the figures had jumped to much higher levels and the general manager had no option but to approve the upgrading.

Several former assistant managers of Stepney had eventually returned to manage that branch, especially in the years following Joe Holmes' retirement. Until I had fallen foul of my local directors I had always harboured thoughts that one day I might have been offered the chance to be promoted to Stepney as manager. I do not know if I would have taken the opportunity, had it occurred, because, although the old building had long since gone and there was a brand new branch sited a few doors up the Commercial Road, the type of business was no longer to my liking. Nonetheless, the offer would have been very flattering. The irony, however, was that when I retired from Basildon, I was succeeded by John Hughes, who had been *promoted* from his position as manager of Stepney branch!

When I had left Stepney, I had in no way escaped from the Jewish orthodox community business. Many of them had brought their accounts to Westcliff, but I had been very selective in which ones I would accept. It was amazing that none of them would give a second thought about driving from Stamford Hill all the way to Westcliff to see me about business, which was always done on a face-to-face basis. Although communication through the post or by telephone was common, this was usually only for enquiries about the accounts or about repayments, especially if they had fallen into arrears. All new lending propositions were discussed in the office and often my callers would take the opportunity to combine their visit with attending an auction of property within the borough of Southend-on-Sea, which often led to further business. Those who did bring their accounts to me were my friends, and I was always glad to see them, and even the dreaded Mr G managed to persuade me to open an account for him. When I say that they had brought their accounts to Westcliff, I do not imply that they had transferred them from Stepney. They would never do that; they would simply create some new limited companies and open the accounts of those companies with me. When I moved on to Basildon the same thing had occurred. It depended on whether or not the new manager at Westcliff had wished to retain their business. If he had decided not to keep the accounts they had been transferred to Basildon, but if he had decided to keep them, accounts for new companies were opened in Basildon. Few managers in the country branches wanted these accounts as they felt the same way as I had felt when I had been so pleased to escape from Mr G. After I had become accustomed to these very shrewd but friendly business men and their ways and customs, my attitude had changed. I had also wanted to ensure that Basildon had a good mix of businesses from across the spectrum, and there was a place in our portfolio for this type of business, provided that we were selective.

The customer base at Basildon grew and grew, mainly through the contacts that we had made by courting the accounts of the professionals, the solicitors and accountants, in particular. Probably the best business to come to the branch was introduced by A W Mudd & Co, chartered accountants. The business had been started by Tony Mudd and his delightful wife, Janet, in the back room of their small house in the East End, but by the time I came to know them the business had grown and they had their own modern suite of offices in Billericay. Tony was not a qualified accountant but had passed the exams of the Chartered Institute of Secretaries. He had insisted upon his partners and employed accountants all being chartered accountants, so that the practice qualified to be chartered accountants. There was no doubt that, despite his lack of a qualification in accountancy, Tony was probably the most capable of his firm, and guided by his extraordinary entrepreneurial skills, the firm flourished.

A W Mudd and Co introduced some excellent accounts to us, but the true benefit from our association was the fact that if any of these accounts ever became troublesome, Tony and his partners always ensured that the bank would not lose money. I shall not pretend that I did not have at least a couple of sleepless nights over any of these accounts, but all had come right in the end. When one is trying desperately to put on business in order to turn around a loss-making branch and to find ways of making it achieve its full potential, some risks must be taken, but one has to avoid being foolhardy. Amongst the excellent accounts that came from the Mudd stable, was a company named IAD Limited, which was run by John Shute and his wife, Yvonne. The initials IAD stood for International Automotive Design. They were motor car designers and had contracts all over the world from Mazda in Japan to Ford and General Motors in the USA. In the case of Mazda, they had been contracted to design a new saloon in its entirety, but in other cases they might be designing only one small section of a vehicle. I took every opportunity to visit their several workshops and design centres on a large industrial site in Worthing.

What I saw at their numerous workshops and offices amazed me. There were complete clay models being created of new motor cars, and there were new vehicles, designed by competitors, which had been completely stripped to the chassis in order that IAD could keep right up to date with the latest technology being used world-wide. It was necessary for the company to have several separate workshops because they needed absolute secrecy for the work that they had in hand for one company, kept discreetly away from what they were doing for another. If the representatives of, say, Ford were to call to inspect how the work on their vehicle was progressing, they had to be prevented from seeing what work was in hand for their competitors.

It was fascinating, but it all came to a head around 1987 when IAD had been nominated as one of the top five British companies for growth and enterprise. The success of the company had already been recognised earlier when it had been awarded the Queen's Award for Exports. On the day of the award, representatives of the five chosen companies were invited to the presentation, which was to be made at a ceremonial lunch at the Savoy Hotel in London, and John and Yvonne had kindly included me in their party. Before the meal and presentation, I was standing at the bar to purchase pre-lunch drinks, when I was rather roughly elbowed aside by another guest who was with one of the other parties. I looked round to see who had pushed in so rudely, and I came face to face with a well-built middle-aged man with a flushed face, which I recognised immediately. It was none other than Robert Maxwell, who, at that time, was head of the Mirror Group of newspapers! After the lunch came the presentations of the awards.

Unfortunately for IAD the top award went to Anita Roddick for the world-wide success of her Body Shop group, and the ceremony ended after she had made her speech in acceptance of her award.

Just before I retired from the bank, IAD became involved in a consortium, led by the Merchant Banking arm of a Scottish bank, to finance a project for a giant Soviet motor manufacturing plant based in Lvov, in the Ukraine, which was then an integral unit of the USSR. At the time, the plan had been to help the economy of the USSR by the manufacture of a van to rival the Ford Transit, but slightly larger and for which there was thought to be a niche in the market.

There were other banks in the consortium besides the Scottish bank, and the Midland Bank Group were certainly amongst the participants. Had Barclays decided not to join in, I think that the Midland Bank would have taken over the IAD account. The news of this project had come as a shock to me, because the company had said nothing, and there had been no indication of its intentions in its financial projections, which had earlier been submitted to the branch. The first that I had heard of it was when my regional office approached me. The corporate director, who assisted branches with business development, seemed to find fault with the fact that I was unaware of what was afoot. Shortly afterwards I attended a meeting of the consortium at the Moscow Narodny Bank in London.

I was not happy at the idea of a company with the very limited capital base of IAD committing itself to such a multi-million pound scheme. I expressed my reservation to my regional office, but since the whole project was to be guaranteed by the Soviet government, it was felt that there was little risk. At that time, nobody had, or perhaps few could have foreseen the collapse of the Soviet Union. I retired before this project had really got started, and I have not enquired what had been its fate following the break-up of the USSR, or how members of the consortium had fared but, unfortunately, during the exceedingly damaging recession of the early 1990s IAD was put into liquidation.

Tony and Janet Mudd in the meantime had gone from strength to strength. They had acquired Stockwell Hall, a moated manor house of fourteen bedrooms, stables and a swimming pool, situated just outside Billericay. It was quite a contrast to the three-bedroomed "semi" where their business had started. Later they had gained a certain amount of national fame when they had lost a much publicised libel case at the Old Bailey brought against them by the well-known MP, Mrs Teresa Gorman. The case concerned a pamphlet that Tony had circulated around the constituency lampooning Mrs Gorman just prior to an election. Substantial damages had been awarded against Tony and Janet, but the Court of Appeal subsequently drastically reduced these damages.

Another of the very progressive customers at Basildon was George Jacobs. George, together with his three sons, ran South Essex Motors Limited, which was the largest Ford dealers in the county.

George and his brother, the latter no longer with the firm by the time that I met George and his sons, had originally owned the famous Canterbury Sidecars Company in Leytonstone. The Canterbury had been regarded as the Rolls Royce of motor cycle sidecars. They had sold that business and had started South Essex Motors in Basildon on the creation of the New Town. The business had grown rapidly, and they had later taken a factory on the main Burnt Mills industrial site to convert tractors manufactured by the local Ford Tractors Plant into a long-wheel-based version for export. Terry Jacobs, one of the sons, ran this unit. Another son, Clive, was a chartered accountant, who had trained with A W Mudd & Co. Once he was satisfied that the company was on a proper financial footing and had the right financial accounting systems established, Clive left to set up his own accountancy practice in the Loughton area. The family had separate property interests and kept another account with Basildon branch for this purpose.

George was, rather like Joe Holmes, a unique character. He was Jewish by birth, but neither George nor his sons were Jewish by religion, or so it appeared. Now and again George and I would clash, but we both had respect for each other, and George had realised that I always put the interests of my customers first, a habit of which my superiors did not always approve. No bones were ever broken between George and myself as a result of our occasional brushes.

George was a great entertainer, but always for the purpose of promoting South Essex Motors. The company would hold open evenings in their showroom and offices, and many celebrities would be invited with the purpose of mingling with the guests. Footballers were top of George's list, and as he was a Tottenham Hotspurs' supporter, one of his most regular celebrities was Ray Clements, the Spurs and England goalkeeper. The family also owned Bugatti's night club in Brentwood, and on the opening night we met Glen Hoddle and other well-known footballing stars.

Tony Mudd and others, including George Jacobs, had belonged to an industrial group, which was associated with the local Conservative Party. The late Bob McCringle was the local MP in those days, and he would organise parties to go for dinner in the dining rooms of the House of Commons. On these occasions Bob McCringle would arrange for senior members of the Tory shadow cabinet to join the party and they would chat with the members and guests over pre-dinner cocktails and then address the gathering after the meal. These events were really fund-raising evenings for the coffers of the Conservative Party. Later, after the 1979 general election, the shadow ministers had become ministers of the Crown. Amongst those with whom we had mingled were Willie Whitelaw, the late Lord Whitelaw, John Selwyn Gummer and several others. Often their presence was interrupted by the division bell, when they would be forced to dash into the chamber to vote, but they would always return afterwards.

I attended several of these evenings, usually hosted by a different customer, including Tony Mudd and George Jacobs. On one particular occasion, George had taken me plus a senior executive of the Ford Motor Company to one of these evenings. The head office of Ford Tractors was also in Basildon – in Transit House, just across the road from South Essex Motors. The three of us had travelled to the Palace of Westminster in George's chauffeur-driven Rolls Royce. On the way, we had stopped at his home in Chigwell in order to pick up Terry. The evening had gone very well, but there had been two interruptions for divisions, and by the time the speakers had finished, George was getting desperate. His intention had been that we should go for drinks at a prestigious gaming club in the West End where he was a member. Unfortunately, the law required the club to close by eleven p.m. The last thing that either his other guest or I needed was any more drink to supplement generous supply of wines and liqueurs that had been heaped upon us, before and with our meal, but George had been adamant. We were rushed to the car, and Terry sat in the front giving authority to the chauffeur to drive through all red traffic lights. On arrival Terry dashed out of the car and into the bar. It was about two minutes to the regulatory time for the bar to close, although the club would remain open until the early hours of the next morning. Being a gaming club, roulette and backgammon and such were being played in the casino, upstairs. The only way to get another drink, after the bar had closed, was to wait for breakfast to be served at one a.m. and provided breakfast was taken, more drinks could be consumed. Breakfast was even lower on my list of priorities than another drink!

When we entered the club, Terry was lining up two drinks for each of us on the bar before it closed. Standing beside the bar was a small rather insignificant elderly man in his overcoat. It was obvious that he had consumed quite a few drinks during the course of the evening, and although he was not particularly merry, he was a trifle unsteady on his feet and swayed slightly. George apparently knew him well.

"Good evening, Joe. Can I get you a drink before the bar closes?" he asked.

Before Joe could reply, a woman's voice interceded and an elderly lady, evidently the wife of the poor man, came over to our party.

"Now come on, Joe. You've had more than enough for this evening!" she said, looking pointedly at George Jacobs, and with that she had gently led the tipsy gentleman away, as he feebly protested, and tried to pass back his farewells.

I then learned that this gentleman had been none other than Joe Coral, whose name stood above the windows of so many betting shops.

It was not before three a.m. the following morning that I had crept into our bedroom, with my shoes in my hand, in order not to disturb Joyce, but I need not have bothered. "You're home, at last!" she uttered in an accusing manner as she turned over to go to sleep again.

One day there was an attempted robbery of cash from the Security Express van, but fortunately the robbers had made a drastic mistake. They had attacked the courier on his return journey from the bank to his van, when he had only a bag full of empty sacks, having just delivered notes *to* the branch. The robbers had obviously thought that he was collecting notes *from* the branch. The raid should have acted as a warning to Security Express. Whenever they came to the branch, situated in a pedestrian precinct, they would park the van in the service area behind the branch and the adjacent shops. The courier then had to walk alone a distance of some thirty yards through an alleyway, between the shops on either side, on to the main pedestrian walkway to the bank. It was not far but it meant that the courier had to pass out of sight of the van driver.

One day, I was interviewing a customer who was rather a time-waster, when there was a loud bang and quite a few shouts. I had tried to end the interview, but my customer would have none of it. Fortunately my assistant manager, Bruce Foxall, had been able to go to the doorway on the ground floor. He then came back upstairs to my room, and after excusing himself to my customer for the interruption he had requested me to go into his adjacent room straight away. At this my customer had fortunately taken the hint and departed.

When I passed into Bruce's room, I found an elderly man sitting at Bruce's desk.

"I got it!" he exclaimed, "I got it!"

Bruce then explained to me what he had discovered when, very fortunately, he had gone to the front door. In the event of a raid our messenger had been instructed to close the front door and not to allow anyone in or out, until instructed otherwise. On this occasion, the messenger had responded immediately, but when Bruce had arrived at the plate glass front door, he had found the messenger standing there. The elderly gentleman was pleading to be let in, and was waving the Security Express bag, full of cash to the value of twenty-five thousand pounds, and crying out, "Let me in! I've got the money!"

"No!" the messenger was saying, "I have my instructions not to let *anyone* in or out!"

Bruce had reacted promptly. "For goodness sake let him in!"

"Well, if you say so!" said the messenger, and he had reluctantly opened the door.

As I was listening to this story, the first cashier came to the room to advise us that some bystanders who knew the old chap, were worried because he had a heart condition and they thought that he should take some medication. We arranged for water to be brought, and he swallowed a couple of his tablets that he carried in his pocket.

"May I make a phone call?" he asked as he looked at me. I naturally thought that he wanted to telephone his wife in case the news should get home before he did, and that she might worry.

I indicated that he should go ahead but, to my astonishment, once he got through to the number he was dialling, instead of explaining to his wife what had happened, he burst out, "*Daily Express* newsdesk? Well put me through to X, I have a hot story for him!" It turned out that he had retired from the *Daily Express* only a short time before this incident.

We had a strict rule in the bank that, immediately after a raid or some other emergency, we were to telephone Head Office Inspection Department and give a full report. *Under no circumstances* were we to speak to anybody, especially not to the media. Anybody from the press or radio were to be referred to the Press and Public Relations Office, who would issue a prepared statement as soon as all the facts were known.

I felt that we were in deep trouble, and I immediately telephoned the office of the chief inspector and reported the incident in full. Fortunately the inspector taking my call saw the funny side and laughed heartily. Except for the usual formalities, we heard no more from Inspection Department about the incident. For the rest of that day our telephones were almost entirely blocked with incoming calls from the news agencies.

I was then fully informed of the remarkable story of the courage of this elderly gentleman. Apparently, the Security Express courier was returning to his van with a sack of notes for return to the Bank of England for destruction, being unfit for re-issue. The robbers attacked the courier in the alleyway, but when he resisted, one of the robbers shot him in the leg with a sawn-off shotgun. Another of the gang then grabbed the cash bag out of the courier's grasp, but in the mêlée to escape from the crowd all around him, he held the bag above his head. Our old gentleman had done no less than to snatch the bag from him and run to the bank door, where he had come up against our redoubtable messenger. The rest of the story has been told, except for the fact that the poor courier suffered terrible wounds from the lead pellets fired into his leg from the shotgun and was off sick for many months. Afterwards, the elderly gentleman had tried to claim a reward from the bank without success. The reason was that, once the Security Express courier had signed for the bag and its contents, the cash no was no longer under the control of the bank, and he had to submit his claim to Security Express. I hope that he obtained his due reward from both, Security Express and the *Daily Express*!

Chapter Eighteen

Conclusion

During the course of the last few years of my time in Barclays Bank, I had become a member of our local South East Essex Regional Committee of Chartered Institute of Bankers. The Institute received its charter only a short time before my retirement.

As a committee member, I was occasionally asked to perform certain tasks involving students who were studying for the Institute exams. One of these tasks involved my leading a South-east Essex team in a competition involving all areas in Britain, in an exercise known as "The Banking Game". This game was played through the Institute computer centre that started all teams from a common base in an imaginary branch. It first produced a broadsheet showing all the statistics and facts about the fictitious branch, i.e. its customer base; its staff numbers; its lendings and the value of credit balances held, etc. The team winning the game would be the one that had achieved the highest profit over the period allotted for the duration of the game. The computer processed all the information fed into it by the various teams based upon the policies adopted and the decisions made by each team. It then sent a weekly updated spreadsheet back to each team showing its progress and the state of its profits in comparison with all its opponents. The game was played over several months until, at a given point, the four leading teams were called to the London headquarters of the institute to play off for the title over the day.

Teams had to decide upon various issues such as the length of queues at the counter; how many telephonists were needed to give a speedy response to telephone calls, and lay down an acceptable length of time before answering the telephone. There were a number of other similar considerations to be met. The teams realised that they needed to balance quality of service against the cost of providing that service. Most teams started the game by giving an excellent service and in so doing they built up a sound customer base. As the game came towards its end however, some very shrewd teams suddenly began to reduce their staffing, thus causing their customers to be faced with very long counter queues or to be kept waiting before somebody accepted their telephone calls. Having increased their business substantially at the beginning, they also began to introduce scurrilous commission charges and high interest rates. As a result the profits of these unscrupulous teams soared and they became the finalists.

Of course, we all considered it to be a huge joke, but there is an old adage that says, "There is many a true word spoken in jest!" and, in my opinion this game was a portent of things to come.

It brought back memories of an occasion when I had visited the office of the bank's treasurer, with some other colleagues from our district. After having been shown around the department, we were addressed by the then deputy treasurer, a gentleman who boasted that it was his decision whenever the bank adjusted its Base Rate. Sitting comfortably behind his desk, with his thumbs in the armholes of his waistcoat, and exuding an air of smugness, he declared, "We don't need your branches! I can make more profit by investing in the overnight money market, and with very few overheads. Your branches are just too costly!" He did not expand upon where he would get the money to invest, if not to a large extent through the branches, but I had already realised that the banks would have been delighted to divest themselves of the branch banking system if it should prove at all possible. I think that they are trying to achieve that objective in today's world.

Towards the very end of my career the new order came into being. It began with the dissolution of the local head offices, in much the same way as Henry VIII had dissolved the monasteries. Around September 1987, all managers were called to meetings at their local head offices to be advised of the regrouping of branches into regions. Half of Chelmsford's branches were to go to Cambridge Region, whilst the remainder, including Basildon, were to go into London East and South Eastern Region, or Lesero, as it was more often called. Most of our local directors had received what was commonly known as a "magenta envelope", advising them of their compulsory early retirement terms. There had certainly been a smack of the, "night of the long knives" about the way in which all this had been carried out. Senior local directors had been no less vulnerable than their more junior colleagues had. Some of the luckier local directors, and some assistant local directors, who, by then, were more likely to have been university graduates than hereditary "blue-bloods", found themselves appointed to control the new regional offices.

The New Order was upon us, and almost overnight most of our teachings and beliefs in the ways to conduct a bank were gone, forever. Experience and tact were to count for nothing because the computers with all their suspect benefits and inherent faults were taking over. I shall say no more, other than that I, for one, could not feel at all comfortable with these developments. The emphasis had to be upon selling. It had always been my joke that I had joined the bank because I was no salesman, and I could not have sold a life-jacket to a drowning man! Joe Holmes in his immense wisdom had once expressed his view that the bank held control over the most sought after product of all – *cash*! Those members of the public who wanted cash would always beat a path to the bank's doors.

The world had changed. Greengrocers sold grocery and grocers sold greengrocery. Petrol stations sold everything from bread to houseplants and newspapers, in addition to petrol and oils and suchlike. Supermarkets had taken over from the corner shops, but, in their turn, the supermarkets were being eaten up by out-of-town hypermarkets. We were told that we had to accept change or to go down. I preferred the old way where there was order and everybody had an opportunity to run his or her own business, however small. People could retain their dignity and have no need to turn to the state for help, nor have to take menial jobs and suffer belittlement to their self-esteems.

I was so fortunate that all these changes to banking were to arise within eighteen months of my retirement. I was even more a misfit at the end of my banking career than when it had all begun some forty-three and a half years earlier.

I owe a great deal to Barclays Bank for all the opportunities that it gave me, despite my somewhat quirky character. I was provided with a generous pension to take into my retirement, plus free private health-care, which has proved to be a great benefit over the past few years. My banking career opened many doors for me to meet influential, powerful, skilled and even titled persons whom I could never have expected to have met otherwise. I also owe a great deal to my former headmaster for introducing me to Barclays, although it might easily have been to one of the other clearing banks, and who knows what that might have led to? Would I have left them to volunteer for the Royal Navy, only to return after seven years? There is no doubt that I had enjoyed substantial benefits from the Royal Navy experience. My greatest regret about current-day banking is that the career profile that I was privileged to be able to follow does not exist for the young men and women of today.

THE END

Glossary of Banking Terms

1 *House Cheques*

Cheques drawn upon the branch itself.

2 *Remittances*

The remittances are the cheques drawn on other branches and banks outside the local clearing. They had to be sorted into the various banks, listed and agreed with the waste and then sent off in the Head Office letter bag for transmission to the Clearing House.

3 *Clearing*

This was the name for the bundle of cheques that were drawn upon our branch for the debit of the accounts of our customers. They had been paid in to different branches of all the banks, and were "cleared" through the Clearing House in St Swithins Lane, in the City of London, and posted to us via our head office.

4 *Local Clearing*

Cheques drawn upon other branches of Barclays and/or of other banks within walking distance of the collecting branch. Each bank or branch would attend a Local Clearing, usually at one of the branches, which would be on a rotary basis day-to-day, and exchange cheques. The difference in value between cheques handed over and those received would be cleared by means of a warrant drawn on the bank handing over the smaller value in its exchange with another bank.

Sometimes these local clearings were held twice daily. Postal and Money Orders were also listed under the Local Clearing column in the waste. These items would be exchanged at a post office for cash, in the case of very small amounts or, for larger amounts, for Post Office Warrants, which in turn would be cleared through the Remittances.

5 Waste

"Waste" was the method by which all incoming credits (payments-in) were proved to agree with the lists prepared by the customers paying credits into their bank accounts. These credits could be for "house" accounts, i.e. our branch, or they could be for other branches of Barclays or for any other bank or branch in the country. The waste was processed on the accounting machines by listing all the postal and money orders; the house cheques; the remittances; and finally the cash element in separate vertical columns. The machines had cross-columns that could calculate the correct value of each credit slip and so prove whether or not the customers' sums were right or wrong. Finally the vertical columns provided figures for the agreement of the postal/money orders; house cheques; and remittances, which we juniors had to list on the adding machines, and the cash for the cashiers to prove against their amalgamated till balances.

6 Town Clearing

A special clearing amongst all branches of the clearing banks situated within walking distance of Lombard Street. Branch messengers would undertake this clearing of cheques subject to a strict timetable. Unpaid cheques had to be returned to the presenting bank, through the Clearing House on the same day.

7 Walks

Prior to the adoption of agency arrangements in 1974, all banks and branches of banks outside the main clearing banks, whose premises were situated within the Town Clearing area were allocated a special four-figure Sorting Code (Glossary 8) and all batched together in the remittances. In the City of London, the banks' clearing departments would "walk" round to the offices of non-clearing institutions for presentation for payment. Where the non-clearing bank office was outside the City, the cheques were sent direct by post.

8 Sorting Code Numbers

The number appearing in the top right-hand corner of all cheques. This is the identification number of the particular branch or office of a bank or institution upon which the cheque is drawn.

These code numbers are for the purpose of clearing cheques or similar instruments. It is usual for each branch of a bank to have a six-digit number, broken into pairs of digits. The first pair identify the bank, the second and third pairs identify the branch.

9 General Ledger

The totals of all credit items and of all cheques and other debit items posted daily to each ledger were entered into the general ledger, and a running balance of each ledger would be recorded. The overall sum of all these balances indicated whether the branch was in credit or in debit with Head Office. Some branches held large credit surpluses, whereas other branches could be lending sums totalling much more than the credit balances that it held in its books.

10 Personal Instalment Loans

Designed to "assist customers towards meeting exceptional expenditure, e.g. house decoration and improvements, equipment for a small business man, the purchase of a car, household equipment or smaller non-recurring items". The loans were available on an unsecured basis to creditworthy customers, including those in receipt of regular wages or salary sufficient to meet the instalments as they fell due. In general, the amount of a loan was not to exceed fifteen per cent of the borrower's annual income, after tax. The maximum loan was five hundred pounds and repayable over six, twelve, eighteen or twenty-four months. Interest was to be charged on the original amount of the loan for the full period of the contract, initially at five per cent per annum. Monthly instalments were then calculated on the gross figure. The effect of adding the full interest charge immediately to the loan meant that on average the true rate of interest paid by the borrower was in the region of nine per cent per annum. However, for the first time, the public at large were offered a fixed-rate loan. Nine per cent per annum was also very favourable rate to the bank in those days of relatively low Bank of England lending rates.

11   "Paying the Clearing"

This term referred to a job undertaken mostly by the cashiers but was a task that could be done by any trained member of staff. Before a house cheque was deemed to be paid, whether it had been received through the general or local clearing or paid in over the counter, it needed to be inspected to see that it had been drawn correctly.

The date would be checked. If it were dated over six months before presentation for payment, then it would be considered as "stale" and the answer "Out of date" would be written in the top left-hand corner in blue ink. Similarly, if it was dated in advance at a future date, the "answer", again written in blue ink in the top left hand corner, would be "Post-dated".

The amounts written in both words and figures would be compared and if there was a difference the blue-ink answer would be: "Words and figures differ." Sometimes either the words or the figures would be omitted. In such a case, it was essential to have the amount in writing but usually the cheque would be returned with the answer: "Amount in words (or figures) required."

Another check would be made upon the endorsement of the cheque by the payee. If it did not concur with the name of the payee or was illegible, or, alternatively, missing, the following answers in blue ink would be applied respectively: "Endorsement requires confirmation" or "Endorsement required". The onerous task of checking endorsements ceased in 1957 after the passing of The Cheques Act 1957.

"Uncleared effects" was a blue-ink reply if the drawer had adequate funds to pay the cheque but, some or all of his required balance comprised uncleared funds and the branch was not prepared to pay against them.

The final blue-ink answers concerned the drawers' signatures; if they were missing or were not in accordance with the customer's own signing mandate. Red-ink answers referred only to cheques that had to be dishonoured (returned) because there was insufficient balance on the account to meet them. In such a case, the answer would be "Refer to drawer", or perhaps "Refer to drawer, please represent" where it was anticipated that the drawer would have funds a day or two later. If there were a case of lack of funds plus a technical reason for dishonouring a cheque, then, by the Rules of the Clearing House, the *whole* answer had to be in red ink.

In novels and plays, one hears that a cheque has been returned with the answer "Lack of funds". This should not happen, since it could be construed as divulging information about the drawer's account. However, very few people were ignorant of the purport of the red-ink answers that referred the payee to the drawer.